ROOM FOR
FOOD AN...
STORIES

by Kenneth Randle Landers

This book is dedicated to my dad,
Wayne Landers.

Foreword

Dear Reader:

This is my first collection of fictional short stories that I'm excited to share with you, and I am humbly honored and thankful to the people who encouraged me to write these stories. To acknowledge two to show some gratitude, when I was in high school, my sophomore English class selected my fictional play "Leon on the Invisible Dog" (which was the basis for my short story "Shoe Away" in this collection) for a performance that was filmed, and the teacher of the class Mr. Richard R. Stitt encouraged me which I'm thankful for; also I'm thankful to Manuel Marrero (the editor of Expat Press) for his encouragement and advice, and I'm pleased that my short story "Room for Good Food" first appeared in Expat Press which the title of that short story is also the title and premise for this book.

I have been inspired by different fiction writers such as J.D. Salinger, John Updike, and Saul Bellow, but my writing is unique. In this collection, there are stories about the relationships between humans and animals such as in "The Cat Behind the Curtain," ethics in stories as "Clear Clouds," complex characters like in "Don't Bug Me," philosophy and literature in stories such as "The Sentimentalist," and grief in stories such as "Dry Tears" and "The Hidden Stack." Also, this book is dedicated to my dad, Wayne Landers, and the importance of the father is illustrated in the stories "A Dirt Road to Freedom" and "The Cat in the Woods." There are other themes you can explore in this collection, and each story has meaning that you can interpret for yourself. I got a lot of nourishment from writing this book and hope it is a room of good food for you too.

Sincerely,

Kenneth Randle Landers

Contents

"Room for Good Food"

"I could use some food," I said as I opened the refrigerator.

"Ya, I could use some good food like pretzels," said Sandy.

"I don't have any pretzels. Let's see I guess I'll have a sandwich," I said.

Sandy without hesitation jabbed, "Ya, go ahead and have a sandwich. I know deep down inside you are a sandwich man."

I was used to her quick snark comments and responded by snickering. I said, "What do you want to eat? Here's some left over casserole that I made for you."

"That was very delicious," she said.

"Glad you liked it," I said.

Then she began to break it down like usual, "20% of it was very delicious."

I played along like usual, although I think she serious. I said, "Oh, so you only liked a little bit of it? Why do you do that? Either you like it or you don't? Why are you always breaking things down into percentages?"

She didn't answer my questions and continued analyzing her reaction to the casserole. She said, "Ya, about 50% of it was okay. And, about 30% of it was just nasty."

I didn't want to argue with her and said, "Glad you liked 30% of it. That's more than last time."

"Well," she said and then continued, "I liked it better last time because even though only 7% of it was very delicious, 60% of it was delicious, and 20% of it was okay. That left 13% of it being--"

I interrupted, "I know, 13% of it was nasty, right?"

"No," she said. "I was indifferent to 13% of it. I had no reaction at all to it."

"Which means what?" I asked.

"It means I had 13% no reaction to it," she said.

So, Sandy could be like that. She would say that she was just being honest, but I wondered if she did that just to irritate me or amuse me. And, she often talked with a lisp which I was suspicious of and wondered if she did that to also irritate me or amuse me. She would say, "A shissy-five-yard field goal" when we watched football. Sandy liked football and would often tell me that she is the quarterback. I guess that meant she liked to be the leader. And, when she recited poetry it seemed like the lisp became more pronounced. She liked to recite William Carlos William's poem "This is Just to Say." However, when she would recite it then it sounded like "Thish shez jesh to shay."

As I was making a sandwich Sandy continued to watch me carefully often throwing in comments that if someone was overhearing for the first time would think were snide, but I think she was being serious.

Just then, a big gray cat struts into the kitchen and said, "Your talking woke me up."

"Ya, right. You're here because you smelled food," I said.

The big gray cat said, "No, I heard you talking to Sandy again. There is something wrong when a grown man talks to a big white cat that he knew in childhood. It's time to put away silly childhood games and only talk to me now."

Then Sandy spoke up, "Since pets are not allowed here, there is room here for both of us, but I'm the quarterback, Wanny."

"Shoe Away"

There once was a dog named Leon. He was a big, yellow, white, and brown German Shepherd dog with brown eyes and pointed ears, but nobody could see him because he was invisible. He was a wild dog, meaning he did not have an owner. He lived in a park and would eat scraps that people would throw away in the trash cans. He never could understand why humans would often throw away their food, but at the same time he was glad that they did in order for him to eat their leftovers. Sometimes, he wondered if some people knew he was there and purposely threw away their food so that he could come along and gobble it up after they had left the park.

Leon also loved to play, but because he was invisible he had no friends to play with. This made him sad. So, besides looking for food, Leon also looked for someone to play with. He often would watch other stray dogs playing and would try to join them, but it would only spook the dogs who would start yelping and run away. He was also envious of the other dogs he saw that had owners who would take them to the park to play. He never approached these dogs because he was too timid. Also, he figured if the stray dogs didn't see him, then the dogs with owners wouldn't see him either.

Leon watched the other dogs in the park with owners play different types of games. He liked watching the dogs catch balls and frisbees, and he knew he could do that too if he was given a chance. One time, he saw a man pull up in a pick-up truck to the park with a big husky dog in the back of it. The man had an old shoe tied to a rope and would swing the rope around, and the big husky dog would jump up and catch the old shoe. The big husky dog would chew on the old shoe and try not to let his owner take it back. Eventually, the big husky dog would let go of the old shoe, and the dog's owner would take it back. Then, they would repeat the game again. Although Leon had never played that game before, he knew that was his favorite game.

So, Leon felt sorry for himself because he wanted someone to play with. He knew he was a good-looking dog because he had seen his reflection in the lake, and he thought that he was just as good-looking as the other dogs in the park. Therefore, he didn't know why he was invisible, but he kept hoping someday that someone would see him and want to be his friend to play with.

One day a man in a brown suit and shiny brown shoes with a brief case stopped to sit down on a bench in the park. He sat down and opened his brief case and took out a paper and began to read it. The man was average height, thin and middle-aged, and he had black hair and blue eyes. Leon saw the man and thought the man looked lonely. Leon also was lonely, so he thought maybe the man and he could be friends, if the man could see him. That was always the problem. Nobody ever saw Leon. Leon thought that he would forget about trying to approach the man and began to trot away, but Leon turned back around and went closer to the man. He observed the man some more because he was fascinated by the man. Leon had seen many business men, but none of them looked so lonely as this man.

Leon thought that the man was good-looking for a human and his suit looked expensive, the kind of suit that some people would probably only wear once a year for an important event like a wedding. To say the man was well dressed was an understatement, even the color of his socks matched the color of his suit and shoes, and his watch was golden. Leon noticed that he had no wrinkles in his suit, amazing. No doubt, the man was a dandy. Leon thought how odd it was for a man who looked like that to be lonely. After some speculation, Leon figured the man was probably just having a bad day, and so Leon decided to leave the man to his thoughts.

However, Leon couldn't turn away from the man. He felt compelled to approach the man and try to play with him. He figured he had nothing to lose. What could happen? He was invisible anyways. So, Leon trotted closer to the man and then stood in front of the man for a few minutes to see if the man would notice him; however, the man was still busy reading and never looked up.

"Hey!" said Leon. The man didn't budge. "Hey!" said Leon a second time but only louder. The man still did not move. The man was deeply focused on what he was reading. "Hey!" Leon barked. This time the man looked up and looked around as if he heard something. Leon was hoping that he heard him, but then the man went back to reading. At this point, Leon became very bold and jumped on the man's lap and began licking the man's face.

The man was more than startled and jolted backward, but he tried intensely to appear as if nothing had happened; thus, strangely, he didn't make a sound at first. Instead, the man pushed Leon off his lap and said to himself, "What's happening? I'm hearing voices. I must be losing my mind."

Leon replied, "I'm trying to play with you. You're not hearing voices, and you're not losing your mind. Can you see me now?" However, the man did not answer. Instead, the man took out his paper and began to read again as if nothing had happened.

"I know you heard me? Will you play with me?" asked Leon. Again, the man did not respond, so Leon figured the man really didn't see or hear him; thus Leon walked away.

However, Leon's bold move made him feel more confident, and he could sense the man saw and heard him. He thought that the man was just playing a game with him, so Leon turned around and again approached the man and jumped in the man's lap and began licking the man's face. Again, the man frantically squirmed around on the bench and pushed Leon off his lap, and then the man finally looked at Leon and said to him, "Please leave me alone. I'm trying to get some work done."

"Can you see me now?" asked Leon.

"Yes. Unbelievable! Man!" said the man.

Leon said, "No, I'm a dog. Take it easy man. I promise not to jump on you again to try and play with you."

The man was amazed but not frightened. However, he was more agitated though than amazed, and he slowly stood up as if it was an inconvenience to him and looked down at Leon and said, "Of course I can see you now. Why wouldn't I? Why do you keep attacking me and licking my face?"

"I didn't attack you. I was only playing with you to get your attention," said Leon.

"You don't get someone's attention by jumping on their lap and licking their face," said the man.

"I'm a dog," said Leon.

"Dogs can behave themselves too," said the man.

"Are you an expert on dogs?" said Leon.

"No, but I've seen the dog shows on TV," said the man.

"I've never been in a dog show. I don't even have an owner," said Leon.

"Why don't you have an owner?" asked the man.

"I'm invisible," said Leon.

"There's no such thing as an invisible dog," said the man.

"You're looking at one," said Leon.

"I need to get going," said the man.

The man began walking away, but Leon kept the man's attention by talking.

"Can you come back and play with me sometime?" asked Leon.

"Uh, I don't know. The truth is I don't like dogs," said the man.

"Why not?" asked Leon.

"I'm a cat person," said the man.

"Why?" asked Leon.

"They don't lick people in the face," said the man.

"That's shallow," said Leon.

"I'm also more like a cat than a dog," said the man.

"How so?" asked Leon.

"I'm aloof like a cat," said the man.

"I can see that," said Leon.

"What do you mean?" asked the man.

"You see yourself in cats, so you like cats. You don't see yourself in dogs, so you don't like dogs. You are withdrawn into yourself. That is your comfort zone. In order to see another, then you will need to see outside yourself. That may be uncomfortable, but you might learn something. In other words, get to know a dog," said Leon.

"You're wise for a dog. Okay, I'll come back tomorrow to take you for a walk like a civilized dog just one time. We'll see if a walk in the park teaches me the meaning of life. Sorry, I don't mean to be sarcastic. Meet me at noon at this bench tomorrow. Oh, you probably don't understand time," said the man.

"That's okay. I'll be waiting at this bench all day tomorrow," said Leon.

"Oh, my name is Leonard. What's your name?" asked the man.

"My name is Leon," said Leon.

"Nice to meet you. I'll see you tomorrow," said the man.

"Likewise. See you then," said Leon.

As the man walked away, Leon wondered if the man was real and wasn't just a part of his imagination. Also, Leon was surprised the man agreed to meet with him tomorrow since the man didn't seem too friendly. He thought that perhaps the man just said that to leave the conversation without being rude. Nevertheless, he was ecstatic because that was the first conversation that he ever had with anyone, if the man was real.

The next day right at noon the man was back sitting on the bench waiting for Leon in the same suit and shiny shoes with his brief case but also this time with a leash and a box of pepperoni pizza. Leon approached the man.

"Why do you have a leash?" asked Leon.

"I said I'd take you for a walk. After I put the leash on you, I'll finish my pizza, and then we'll go for the walk. You can wait on the leash like a good dog while I finish my pizza," said the man.

"You didn't say you'd walk me with a leash," said Leon.

"That's how people walk their dogs. Isn't that what you want?" asked the man.

"You can take me for a walk, but no leash," said Leon.

"If you want an owner, you will have to learn to obey your owner," said the man.

"I want a friend to play with, without having to give away my freedom," said Leon.

"It's just a walk," said the man. Then, the man tried to put the leash on Leon, but Leon ran away. The man started talking to himself again out loud, "Silly dog. Why did I agree to meet with him today? I could be getting a lot of work done instead." Then, the man sat down on the bench and took out a slice of pepperoni pizza from the pizza box and began to eat it.

Leon hadn't run off too far though. He watched the man eat the pizza from some bushes. Pepperoni pizza was Leon's favorite type of food. Leon figured if he couldn't eat any of the pizza, then he could at least smell it, so he scooted closer to the man in order to smell the pizza. He usually could find plenty to eat in the trash cans in the park and didn't understand why humans would throw away good food. However, he noticed that humans hardly ever threw away pepperoni pizza. That must be the food that humans love the most he often thought. So, it was always a special treat when he would find some pepperoni pizza in a trash can. He approached the man.

"Can I have some pizza?" asked Leon.

"It's not dog food," said the man.

"Why are you mean?" asked Leon.

"I'm invisible like you," said the man.

"What do you mean?" said Leon.

"I have no friends. People at work ignore me. I'm the hardest and best worker in my company, but others keep getting promoted over me," said the man.

"I knew I could see myself in you," said Leon.

"There's a lot of people that are invisible, so don't think that makes us friends. Since you don't want to go for a walk, after I finish my pizza I'm only gonna get some work done. Please go find a homeless man to play with. I'm sure a lot of homeless people are also invisible," said the man.

"Okay, I know you cats are aloof. I'll leave you alone," said Leon, and he sadly walked off with his tail between his legs. However, again, Leon didn't stay far away. He continued to watch the man eat pizza from a distance.

Leon was angry at how his new friend just treated him. He didn't understand why the man wouldn't share his pizza which made him upset and was also upset at what else the man said. He watched as the man took out another slice of pepperoni pizza and set it down next to him on his briefcase. Leon was angry and hungry. Instead of looking through the trash cans for lunch, he wanted that slice of pepperoni pizza that the man set on the briefcase. So, he decides to steal it. While the man was reading a paper, Leon sneaked up and snatched the slice of pizza off the man's brief case and ran off with it. He ran off far enough behind some bushes to eat it. Then, he dropped the pizza on the ground and got down to eat it. Just before he decided to take a bite out of it, he saw a female dog who was a tall, thin, yellow Labrador with brown eyes walk by him. She was the most beautiful dog that he had ever seen. He wanted to approach her, but he figured she wouldn't see him.

He stood up and continued to watch her for a while. This was enough time for another white and brown stray dog to come along and grab the slice of pizza under him where he stood and run off with it. Leon chased the other stray dog and then jumped on the stray dog which spooked the stray dog enough that the stray dog dropped the pizza, and Leon was able to reclaim the slice of pizza. He went back to the spot where he saw the Labrador dog, but he could not locate her anymore. He won his pizza back from the stray dog, but he lost sight of his dream girl. However, he still didn't eat the pizza. He thought that maybe he'd see her again and then he can still offer her the pizza. He looked around the park for a while, and he then sat down again with his pizza. He began to imagine himself approaching her and offering her the pizza: she heard and saw him, and he gloriously stood before her glowing like a great statue. She accepted the pizza and thanked him for it.

However, he realized that he can't find her, and he is getting famished. So, he looked down at his pizza, but then he began feeling guilty about stealing it from the man. After all, the man was the only person who had ever seen him, and the man said he was like him too. The man was lonely like him, so he felt bad for stealing from the man. And, he also knew that stealing was wrong. Although he was a wild dog, he had morals. He had never stolen food before, and he didn't plan on starting to do that now just because the man was mean to him and he was hungry for his favorite food. He decided that he had been tested, but he had passed the test.

Just after he decided to take the pizza back to the man, he saw the Labrador again. Then, his heart was given an even bigger conflict because he had been wanting to approach her and offer her the pizza. However, he stood his moral ground. It was torture though. He didn't realize doing the right thing could be so difficult. He knew he had to give the pizza back to the man. Also, he knew he had to look away from her or he would change his mind. Thus, he looked away from the Labrador and trotted back to the man.

The man was still sitting on the bench reading his paper. Leon approached the man and dropped the pizza by the man's feet. The man looked down at Leon and picked up the slice of pizza. He looked the pizza over and sarcastically said to Leon, "Just how I like it, with dirt and slobber all over it."

"At least I brought it back. I felt guilty about it. I apologize. Can we still be friends?" asked Leon sheepishly.

"Okay. I realize you are no ordinary stray dog. Since you brought back my pizza, we can be friends. You can have the slice of pizza." said the man.

"Thank you!" said Leon.

"You're welcome! What game would you like to play?" asked the man.

"I wish we could play with an old shoe on a rope. You would swing the rope around, and I would try and jump at it and grab it with my mouth. Then, you would try and take the shoe back away from me. Once I allow you to have it back, then we play the same game again. I have seen an owner play this with his dog," said Leon.

"I don't have an old shoe," said the man. "Wait a minute, I can tie this leash to one of my shoes. It's not an old shoe, but after you chew on it awhile, it will be like an old shoe," said the man.

"That's a new shoe!" said Leon.

"It's okay. Don't worry about it. I want to do something special for you because you brought the pizza back," said the man.

"No, I need an old shoe is what I mean," said Leon.

"Seriously?" asked the man.

"I guess that will have to do," said Leon.

The man shook his head but takes off one of his shiny shoes and ties it to the leash.

"Hey, wait a bit. I have to go bury this slice of pizza in order to hide it. I'm saving it for my dream girl," said Leon.

"I ate the rest of the pizza. I didn't know you were coming back," said the man.

"That's okay. You really don't know dogs do you," said Leon, and then he quickly ran off with the pizza. About five minutes later, he came back.

"Are you ready now?" asked the man.

"Yes. Let's go play!" exclaimed Leon.

The man and Leon went deeper into the park to play with the man's new dress shoe tied to the leash. When they found a good spot in the park, the man swung the leash around, and Leon jumped high and caught it with his mouth. Then, the man tried to take the shoe away from Leon, and Leon growled and wouldn't let the man take it back. Eventually, Leon let the man have the shoe back, and they repeated the game again. They played this game for a while, until the man stopped and took his shoe off the leash and put it back on his foot.

"I got to get going," said the man.

"Will you come back again tomorrow to play?" asked Leon.

"I can't tomorrow. I'm only in town for a couple of days. I'll come back and visit you though in the future sometime," said the man.

"I must say I think I know why you are invisible. I figured you are a quiet gentlemen and people take advantage of you. I know deep down you are unselfish and kind to others, and you would think that would be enough to be noticed and appreciated by others. Unfortunately, it seems like the kind ones often do get unnoticed because people take them for granted and don't appreciate them. You should still be unselfish and kind, but you need to figure out how to get people to notice you just like I was able to get you to notice me. I had to help push you outside of yourself in order to see me. You were too drawn within yourself to at first notice me. You were like the people who don't see you where you work. I have come to realize that we are only invisible if we choose to be," said Leon.

"I didn't use to be invisible. I once had many friends, but things seemed to get too complicated; so I began distancing myself from others in order to make my life simpler. However, I got used to it too much, and then eventually it became who I was. The only problem was I became lonely and others couldn't see me anymore," said the man.

"If you changed before, then you can change again. You have to be bold and assertive, do what it takes without hurting anyone, even if it means not being a gentleman. Get their attention at work. Tell them that they had better start treating you right or you will go work somewhere else. Stand up for yourself and be seen! Say, here I am!" said Leon.

"How can a dog be so wise?" asked the man.

"Never assume you can't learn from someone different than you, even a stray dog like me. Now go get the job you want, and I'll go get my dream girl. Good-bye my friend, Leonard," said Leon.

"Good-bye buddy. I have learned a lot from you. I'll take your advice. Take care Leon," said Leonard. Leonard started walking away.

"Hey Leonard! What type of dog am I?" barked Leon.

"You're a German Shepherd!" yelled Leonard.

"Really! You do know something about dogs after all, not bad for a cat person," barked Leon.

As the man walked away, Leon whimpered. He had just made a friend for the first time, and then his friend had left. However, he knew his friend would be back sometime in the future to play with him. This gave him hope that he would see his friend again in the future which cheered him up some. He was still feeling somewhat down though as he went back over to the bench to see if maybe Leonard was back there. Of course, Leonard wasn't there, but Leon sat on the bench and decided he was going to wait until Leonard returned to play with him. He was very hungry and thought about the pizza that he had buried for the Labrador. He wondered if he would ever see her again and thought that maybe he should go dig it up and eat it for himself. Although he was hungry, what he was given was a fulfillment more than pizza. He found a friend.

Then, Leon saw the Labrador, so he approached the dog. At first, the Labrador could not see him. Then, Leon calmly spoke with confidence in his voice and offered the dog his pizza, and she then saw the beautiful German Shephard standing there glowing like a noble golden statue in front of her, just like he had imagined he should. He introduced himself as Leon. The Labrador said her name was Leona. Each one was bright in each other's eyes. She was also happy to meet him and accepted the pizza that he had dug up to offer her. He didn't tell her that it had been buried, but she could tell the slice of pepperoni pizza had been through a lot of strife. Somehow though, the pepperoni managed to cling to the crust. And, being the gentleman that he was, Leon licked the pizza clean before he served it to his queen. She was grateful and said, "You're so macho Leon," and they walked off together.

"The Cat Behind the Curtain"

"The Ralphy Show. The Ralphy Show. We're gonna getcha, getcha, getcha with the Ralphy Show. There is Ralphy and Raphy too, so here we goo with the Ralll-pheee show!" Dawson sang these words as he opened the window curtains, and there sitting on the window ledge drenched in the sun was Ralphy. Gathered around the window like a shrine were many of Dawson's friends who often came over to his house to see the Ralphy show. Ralphy kept silent and didn't move, showing no reaction to being the star of the production. Dawson's friends stared at Ralphy with awe and anticipation, but Ralphy remained still like a furry statue.

It was silent a bit which complimented the vibe, and then Ralphy spoke, "What do you want?" With that question, the audience roared with laughter. Some of them tried to contain their laughter, but they couldn't.

Dawson replied, "They are here to see your show."

Ralphy replied, "My show? This is your stupid show. I just sit here and you do the talking. Shut the curtains and leave me alone." Ralphy was looking at the floor out of the corner of his eye like he had seen a mouse. Escaping the moment was like a mouse he wanted to catch. When he hunted for a mouse, he would crouch down and remain still. If Dawson saw him and approached him, he would tell Dawson to leave him alone because he was hunting. However, the Ralphy show was different.

"Ralphy, tell my friends what you did today," said Dawson.

"What I did today is beyond their comprehension," said Ralphy.

"Don't be rude," said Dawson.

"What I did today is nobody's business," said Ralphy.

"All you did was sleep," said Dawson.

"I caught a bird," said Ralphy.

"That was yesterday. And you took it in the house and let it fly around," said Dawson.

"You could have told them that on your own," said Ralphy.

"You were showing off. That's cruel," said Dawson.

"I'm a cat," said Ralphy.

"Last week you went number 2 in my closet bedroom and then covered it up with the newspaper you found in the living room. My mom found it and blamed me for it," said Dawson.

"Number 2! Who says that? Is this a show? Or, are you just trying to make me look like a cat in front of your friends?" said Ralphy.

Dawson's friends were always dazzled by the piquancy of the show and at times didn't know whether to laugh or not. Sometimes Ralphy would sing. He loved football, and his favorite NFL team was the Pittsburg Steelers. He liked to sing, "Pittsburg's going to the Super Bowl!" Dawson's friends loved it.

Ralphy still sat still looking forward as if nobody was watching him. He was a natural because he didn't seek attention. His cavalier towards the audience made him calm. And it didn't hurt none that he looked fit for a castle. He was a big, beautiful Siamese cat with white fur, and his face, paws, and tail were black. His hummingbird-like voice was as soothing as his purr, but he wasn't purring at the moment. Often, Dawson would let Ralphy in the house after the rest of the family went to bed, so Ralphy could sleep on Dawson's bed. And, Dawson usually stayed up all night wresting ideas and his faith, and he hadn't forgotten waking up with Ralphy lying on his chest staring at him and purring to welcome him after the night's long journey. And, there were many times Ralphy was the only one Dawson could talk to, and Ralphy wouldn't allow anyone to pick him up except for Dawson.

Ralphy was Dawson's best friend even though Dawson shot Ralphy with a rubber band on his nose. Dawson would sometimes play too rough with Ralphy, and one-time Ralphy's primal instinct had enough; so he lunged at Dawson's face and tore up his face. He got some good scratches in. Then, Ralphy put his head down and waited for the blow. Dawson was first startled in disbelief and then hit Ralphy a few times on the nose and threw him against the wall. Ralphy never did that again, but he thought the punishment was worth it. He would have done that again, but he was loyal to Dawson. When Dawson went off to college, Ralphy often went to his bedroom door and cried.

The Ralphy show was just as entertaining as always. And, at this point in the show, Dawson decided to crank it up some more and said to Ralphy, "Then, the week before last you peed in my mom's face because she wouldn't feed you when you demanded it. What about that?"

"She's my mom too," said Ralphy.

"You're a cat," said Dawson.

"I already said that," said Ralphy.

"Don't be such a--"

Before Dawson could finish his sentence, Ralphy interrupted by saying, "I was adopted, but she's my mom too."

"Then that makes you peeing in her face even more reprehensible," said Dawson.

"I don't try to pretend to be a human. You should stop trying to be funny," said Ralphy.

"If I wasn't funny, then my friends wouldn't come to see the show," said Dawson.

"They come to see me," said Ralphy.

"Ask them whom they come to see?" said Dawson.

"I don't talk to your friends," said Ralphy.

"Why not?" asked Dawson.

"I bet none of them have read Kierkegaard," said Ralphy.

"Kierkegaard?" inquired Dawson.

"I was up all night contemplating *Fear and Trembling*," said Ralphy.

After the Ralphy show, later that night Dawson and Ralphy were putting on a play for the family. Ralphy was dating Raggedy Ann and was the quarterback. Raggedy Andy was his friend, but he had to fight Dapper Dan for Raggedy Ann's attention. Ralphy was a fighter, and as expected he beat up Dapper Dan. He had an advantage because he had claws and fangs. And, Ralphy only wore a mohawk and didn't need clothes like Dapper Dan to be dandy. Ralphy was still the coolest cat in the room just like now.

"Clear Clouds"

It was a dark, cloudy day in January in the Midwest. Verny sat in his office grading papers when the Dean opened his office door and stormed in and stood looking down at Verny and began pontificating, "Kayla Holton's father is putting pressure on me to get you to change his daughter Kayla's grade. Kayla got an F in your class and thinks she should have gotten at least a C. Will you change her grade from an F to a C?"

"No, I can't do that. That's not what she earned, so it wouldn't be fair to the other students or her to change her grade," said Verny.

"These things happen sometimes, and I have to gently coerce some teachers sometimes in order to make some people happy. I'm sure you understand," said the Dean.

"No, like I said, that wouldn't be right. I can't do that," said Verny.

"You're young and naïve. You don't understand how it works. Sometimes the end justifies the means, and we need to make Kayla's father happy. People like him help keep this college open and give us pay checks. You don't want to rock the boat do you? You are still idealist, but you will learn in time. I will mentor you and show you the ways of the world," said the Dean.

"I'm not naïve about the world, but this is a Christian College. I expected those in power here to be honest and do the right thing," said Verny.

"Kayla claims she put all her make-up work because she was sick under your door in a big brown envelope," said the Dean.

"She did put one page that had a few words on it which didn't make sense in a folder under my office door. However, it wasn't her make-up work. I never received her make-up work, and she never asked me about it. If she has a copy of her make-up work right now then I will grade that. Did she save her work?" asked Verny.

"Kayla says her work was saved on her computer and her computer crashed and she would need to get a code from the government in order to retrieve her work on it. However, she says she can't get a code from the government," said the Dean.

"If she can't show me her work, then how can I grade it? She will need to accept the grade that she earned," said Verny.

"I'll tell Kayla what you said, but I don't think she will accept it and neither will her father," said the Dean as he walked out the office door.

The Dean was a very tall and sleek man with grey hair in his sixties, and he was well dressed in an expensive black suit; and he was worldly – had worked for big companies in his past in Los Angeles and Miami. He thought that being Dean in a small town in the Midwest would be like a cushy retirement for him, but he found it to be stressful and acted like it was a burden to him. He also underestimated the cold weather which also contributed to his ill temperament. He prided himself on being well-connected and often bragged about all the famous people that he knew. Verny and some of the other teachers didn't like to be around him much because the Dean liked to control the conversation and also name drop a lot. The Dean said he was friends with a lot of famous actors in Hollywood. This didn't impress Verny, but the Dean thought it would because Verny was young. The Dean often said to Verny, "You're just a kid."

It is true that Verny was young for a professor, and those who did not know him thought he was a student. He was in his late twenties, and one time he pretended to be a student on the first day of one of his classes that he taught. He was sitting in the classroom at the beginning of the first day of the class with the rest of the students waiting for the professor to arrive, and then he finally got up and said, "Hello, I'm your teacher." Verny was good natured. He was short and bulky with black hair, built like a linebacker; however, he was gentle and humble and didn't like trouble. However, he was wise enough to know that being honest and doing the right thing in the world can cause conflict.

A week passed, and the Dean paid Verny another visit to his office. The Dean said, "Kayla won't accept her grade and wants to pursue this. Will you compromise?"

"No, like I told you, it wouldn't be fair to the other students, and it wouldn't be fair to Kayla either -- to give her a grade that she didn't earn. That wouldn't be right," said Verny.

Then the Dean became livid and began speaking louder and faster, "You are selfish. If you would have been proactive then we wouldn't be here right now. It is sixty percent your fault and forty percent her fault. Other teachers have compromised in this type of situation. I'm trying to mentor you. Will you compromise?"

"No, I can't compromise. It's not about me. I have to do the right thing," said Verny. The Dean was standing as he usually did in Verny's office looking down at Verny while Verny sat at his desk. The Dean liked to stand and use his height as an advantage to help him try to dominate. Then, Verny stood up and walked over to him and looked up right into the Dean's eyes and said, "You are wrong, and I can prove it." The Dean was bewildered. He was not use to any teacher standing up to him. The only people he feared were those who had more power than him like the Holtons.

"Okay, Kayla and you will go before a committee who will hear the case and make a decision," said the Dean.

"Why can't you make the decision? I'll show you my gradebook," said Verny.

"No, I don't want to see your gradebook. The committee will make the decision," said the Dean and walked out and slammed the office door, knocking some books off the top of one of Verny's bookshelves.

About two months passed by, and the Dean continued to try and put pressure on Verny to change Kayla's grade from an F to a C; but Verny kept saying that he couldn't do it. The Dean would call and talk to him about it over the phone and even had a meeting in his office with Verny about it. Each time, Verny still said he couldn't change Kayla's grade. So, there was a hearing in March. The committee was selected by the Dean and was made up of other professors. The Dean wanted to take the pressure off of himself and try to make the committee responsible for the decision. Kayla's father was a patron of the college and one of the wealthiest men in the state of Ohio. Going and excelling at Westbank College was a tradition in Kayla's family, and she had several relatives there. Her uncle Dr. Bruce Holton taught there and was head of the Bible Department but wasn't on the committee. Another teacher and friend there had confided in Verny that he had given Kayla a better grade than she earned in his class in order to not rock the boat. He told Verny that it would be a good idea for Verny to do the same, but Verny had to do what was right. He had to follow his heart.

The day of the hearing arrived in March, and Verny showed the committee his gradebook; and each committee member looked over the gradebook and heard what was said, and it was clear to each of them that Kayla earned an F in the course. Thus, they ruled in favor of Verny, and Kayla's grade stayed an F. During the hearing, Verny read a letter that Kayla had written and given him on the last day of class when students took the final. In this letter that Kayla admitted to the committee that she wrote, Kayla explained that the absences she had in Verny's class were not because she was sick but because she didn't like the class. She said that instead of going to class she enjoyed taking hot showers. Verny told Kayla during the semester that she could make-up the work she missed from being absent, giving her three weeks during the semester to make it up because Kayla told him that she had been sick. However, Kayla's letter showed that she had lied about being sick. Also, in the letter, Kayla said she didn't like Verny's class because Verny talked about Vogue magazine too much. Verny explained to the committee that he never talked about Vogue magazine in class and didn't subscribe to it and never had. One of the committee members was trying not to laugh.

Kayla was a pretty, tall, slim, blonde girl who was on the college volleyball team. Many of the Holtons had not only excelled in academics but also athletics at Westbank College. Dr. Bruce Holton had been an All-American wide receiver in football there. Before the hearing Kayla didn't look too concerned about it. She was thinking that because of who she was that she would get her way. The argument that Kayla gave to the committee at the hearing was her story that the Dean had already told Verny about which was she didn't have a back-up saved of any of her make-up work because her computer crashed and she needed a code from the government in order to retrieve it but couldn't get a code from the government. The committee resented the Dean for not looking at Verny's gradebook and hearing the case and making the decision by himself. The case was clear and didn't need a committee hearing, and they knew that. It was obvious to the committee that the Dean was trying to avoid taking responsibility for the decision.

However, after word was out that the committee ruled in Verny's favor and Kayla's grade remained an F, the Dean told others that he always supported Verny and knew all along that Verny was right. The Dean also told Verny that he wanted to take him to dinner and introduce him to some of his famous friends. He wanted to mentor Verny more now than ever since Verny was seen as a hero. However, Verny didn't accept the Dean's offer and also decided to leave the college after the school year because he didn't want to work there anymore. The college had a going away party for Verny whom was their hero, and as Verny drove out of town in May he was wondering if Kayla had learned her lesson. He had heard that Kayla had also tried the same thing before and was not able to change her grade when she was in high school, so he doubted if Kayla had learned her lesson. Verny thought it was a shame that privilege can corrupts a person, and he had seen it there not just in Kayla. He also thought about some of the hypocrisy he had seen there at a Christian college which made him wiser about the world. He knew that some people use Christianity to wear as a mask to try and hide their corruption. However, he also already missed many good people there that he loved. And, he knew that what he had done was good and rare and felt an indescribable lightness of being.

"No Plan Arrives First"

After my buddy Frank and I finished watching the movie *Midnight in the Garden of Good and Evil*, I said to Frank, "Have you ever been to Savannah, Georgia?" He said, "No." And, I said, "Neither have I. I'd like to visit there. Do you want to go?", and he answered, "Yes." So, we both got up and went to Savannah, George.

We left at night and took his car from San Angelo, Texas and took turns driving and slept while the other dove. We drove straight through from San Angelo, Texas to Savannah, Georgia. The roads where smooth until we got into Mississippi, and then they were smooth again when we entered Alabama. When we got to Savannah, Georgia, we drove around a little, and it looked like an empty, old town, not quite like it seemed to be in the move *Midnight in the Garden of Good an Evil*. So, we drove up to Myrtle Beach and got out and looked at the Atlantic Ocean for a while and then took off again. We stayed at different motels on our trip, and on the way back we went through the Great Smoky Mountains and could see why they were called the Great Smoky Mountains, as I reached out the car window to try and grasp the fog.

Frank is a tall, skinny redhead, and I'm short and stocky with brown hair. Though we looked a lot different from one another, we were both restless and went wherever and whenever we felt like it. One night it would be Austin, another night it would be San Antonio, another it would be Houston. We didn't plan it. Usually, we would take off at night because someone suggested it, and so we'd jump in Frank's car or my pick-up truck and go. We would spend all night roaming when we got there, Sixth Street in Austin, the River Walk in San Antonio, walking the streets of Houston at 3 a.m. It happened that way too when we went to New Orleans. We took Frank's car and drove a long way on the beach of the Gulf of Mexico, and then we jumped out and went swimming in the Gulf. In the water, we could see fish jumping around us, and Frank said, "There's a reason fish are jumping out of the water. It means that they are being chased by a predator." It was eerie not being able to see through the muddy water.

In Galveston, we found a public beach to go swimming. I reached down to feel the ocean floor and pulled up a hand full of oil. And, I wore my tennis shoes without socks when I went swimming there, and my feet got very inflected. So, we found a nearby drug store, and I bought some medical supplies; and Frank did the best he could to doctor up my feet. It made walking around though a challenge since my feet were rebelling, but we still went wherever we wanted. And, as we left Galveston and drove toward Louisiana, we stumbled upon a nude beach. We saw a side road and decided to take it. I said, "Watch, it will be a nude beach." And, just as I finished saying that we drove up along the nude beach. There was a mix of men and women, and the men were giving us dirty looks; and the women were smiling at us. Then, as we left that nude beach we drove up along a new one, but this time it was all men; and they were smiling at us.

We camped way down in the swamps of Louisiana in a little tent. I was hoping we wouldn't be visited by alligators wanting to join us on our trip. And, it was in the middle of July, so the heavy hot humidity and thick masses of mosquitos were bigger foes to me than my aching feet. The little tent was cramped and too hot to sleep in, so I couldn't sleep; and I went and tried to sleep in Frank's car, still couldn't sleep but felt safer in the car away from the alligators. Frank was acting strange too that night and saying things that night that didn't make too much sense. Perhaps it was the heat or the mosquito spray. Earlier that night he had went to put some mosquito spray on and accidently sprayed himself in the face. He started talking about how people are basically like ducks, and I was a green duck. The green duck was the cool duck among the ducks because it was green. He pointed out my green eyes to help support his argument. He said that I had a big ego because I was like a green duck; however, he said I had more good in me that overcompensated my big ego. I didn't appreciate being judged like that, especially in the middle of the night in the swamps of Louisiana in July. And, later he apologized and said it was the mosquito spray talking and not him. He said he was really high from the mosquito spray that he accidently sprayed in his face.

When we got to New Orleans, we walked all over the city, and looking back now I don't know how I was able to do that considering my infected feet at the time. However, caught up in the adventure and the crowds and novelty of the city offered me new sensations that overcompensated my painful feet. I suppose there was something to Frank's theory about something good overcompensating something not so good. We both liked the strangeness of the city, and I could see why so many writers had been drawn to it. The city was old but new to us. Frank and I were starving for adventure and exploring new sensations. At night when we were driving down in the Swamps of Louisiana, we would roll the window down and try to describe the smells. The smell of swamp water mixed with the pure lush greenery was a sweet aroma. And, a vivid picture of the sleepy muddy Mississippi River remains in my mind.

One night Frank said to me, "Hey, let's go hike the Brazos River." And, I said, "Okay." So, like usual, away we went in his car. We also had another friend with us this time. When we got there, we jumped out and started hiking along the river. A man saw us and approached us and said, "This is my property. You better get out of here! I'm gonna go get my gun." And, so we took off running. I ran as fast as I could, and my heart was pounding like a drum which shook my whole being. Nobody said a word on the way back to San Angelo, and I was angry at Frank for a while. I thought it was reckless of him to take us there to hike on private property in Texas. Although, it wasn't too long after that Frank called me up and asked me if I wanted to go hike the Guadalupe mountains, and I said yes. So, away we went again. On that trip we just didn't hike the Guadalupe mountains, but also the Davis Mountains and Big Ben. We also walked across the Rio Grande river and walked around the border of Mexico and back. It was one adventure after another with Frank, and we almost always got along well. I was an English major, and he was Biology major; so we weren't competitive with one another. I didn't mind him leading a hike, and he didn't mind me talking about poetry.

A time where Frank really proved his loyalty to me was a night when him, myself, and another friend went to Burger King. As we were leaving in the parking lot, a group of guys pulled up in a truck. One of the guys looked at me and flipped me off and said, "Fuck you." I jumped out of the car and went inside the Burger King and challenged the guy to come outside and fight. I stood there holding the door, and he took out a knife and said that he could kill me. I said to him, "If so, I will try and take as many of you with me as possible." He and nobody from his group stepped outside the door. And, during this episode, Frank got out of the car and stood beside me. He was ready to back me up if he had to. Our other friend stayed in the car. Frank was mad at me for a while about that but not for too long perhaps because it made things even with the incident hiking along the Brazos River.

The other night I called up Frank to see how he was doing. I hadn't talked to him in over a year, and it has been many years since college and our adventures. He has a wife and children now with a lot of responsibility. He is not quite as carefree as I remember him to be back in college when we would go wherever and whenever we wanted. However, as I was talking to him, he was running. I said to him, "Sometime in the future, I'll go visit you in Texas, and we can go on a road trip and listen to Joe Walsh." He said, "That would be great, Hughie."

"Pizza and Beer"

I was twenty and gone home for the summer to work at the local grocery store, and I hadn't seen my big brother Huxley yet. He played football at USC. I came home from work, and the house was empty; but the refrigerator was stocked with beer. I knew Huxley was home. Mom and Dad were out of town, and my big brother Huxley and his football buddies were there with their girlfriends for the weekend. When Huxley and his gang arrived, we went into the backyard and used a gas funnel to drink one beer after another. Trying to keep up with Huxley and his friends with drinking was impossible, but I tried my best. Huxley use to say, "If you can't hang with the big dogs, you better stay on the porch." And, he meant that literally too that time him and his gang visited because there was a porch in our back yard.

I first drank when I was sixteen when I went to visit Huxley at USC. Huxley had some Tang and Everclear in his apartment that I mixed. Huxley thought it was cool to get his little brother drunk and also take me along to bars and parties with his football buddies. I was a scrawny little sixteen-year-old, and here I was hanging out with starting linemen for USC. I wasn't the smoothest when talking to the older ladies. They just assumed I was a college student who looked really young. I told one girl that I was majoring in Liberal Science which was no such thing, and she looked confused. When Huxley turned twenty-one, he gave me his fake ID, but Huxley didn't look like me. I had dark, brown hair, and Huxley had blond hair, almost white. Plus, I was a lot smaller than him, so I tried to use the fake ID; and it didn't work. The guy at the cash register looked at it and said, "No, that's not you." So, I gave the fake ID to a friend who looked more like Huxley, and it worked for him, even though my friend was younger than me. It also didn't help that I looked younger than I was.

I have always had a boyish look. Tonight, I was trying to buy some non-alcoholic beer and got carded, and I'm in my fifties now. The lady at the counter asked me if I was over 21, and I said, "Yes." Then, the police officer standing there said, "I don't believe you. You better card him." So, I took out my ID and showed it to the cashier.

My high school friends envied me for having a big brother who played football for USC and also how I would go down there and party with him and his buddies. The town I grew up in is very small and about five hours north of Los Angeles. So, I'd go down on a weekend and stay with Huxley after a home game and go out on the town Saturday night. It was strange though going to different parties and seeing the players I admired getting drunk. I watched the starting QB who just earlier that day had thrown three touchdowns stumble around in someone's backyard and lip synch Motley Crue's ballad "Home Sweet Home." On Sunday, I'd take the long trip back up north completely hung over, and on Monday morning I'd tell my high school friends all about my adventure that weekend. I was the first out of my friends to drink. One of my friends showed his envy more than the others and would make comments like, "Hey, my little brother Kyle plays for UCLA." Or, he'd say, "You're just an All-American boy. Go eat at McDonalds!" We didn't even have a McDonalds in our small town, so eating at McDonalds would have been a step up. One of my friends made Huxley mad because he was a UCLA fan and made a comment to Huxley about UCLA beating USC. Huxley was home visiting, and I wanted him to buy beer for my friends and me; but my friend's comment annoyed him. Huxley took me aside and told me that he didn't want to buy beer for my friend who made that comment about UCLA beating USC. He also told me that I needed to tell my friend to shut up. Huxley took the rivalry between USC and UCLA very seriously.

I visited Huxley one time during the summer, and he took me to a party in someone's backyard. He introduced me to one of his friends who was a tennis player, and the tennis player looked at me and said,

"Boy, you sure were short changed." I responded by cussing him out and threatening to beat him up. Huxley was angry at me about it and took me to the front of the house and chewed me out and took me back to his apartment and left me there the rest of the night. The next day Huxley told me that he'd give me another chance. We were going to meet up with the tennis player again and some of his football friends later that night. It was around noon on a Saturday that him and I started drinking early. He had bought a bottle of Vodka and a twelve pack of beer. We went and got in the jacuzzi in the apartment complex where he lived and drank that all up. Then, we went out on the town.

Since he was a USC football player, we could get in anywhere for free and were given free drinks. I was nineteen and underage of course, but they would let me in the bars because I was with Huxley. Usually, one of Huxley's teammates was working the front door. We went to this one bar, and this huge guy, working the front door, said, "Hey Hux, come on in." Huxley said, "This is my little brother Ronny." And, the big guy said, "Nice to meet you Ronny, come on in." The big guy didn't even ask me for ID. Inside, Huxley kept giving me drinks, and I'd drink whatever he gave me, drinks called all kinds of crazy names like "Cowgirl Cock Sucker" and "Sex on the Beach." And, to top it off later that night at a barbeque drinking party outside at an apartment complex, I was trying my best to talk coherently to people, and I couldn't walk straight.

I had spent some time that night talking to a USC cheerleader, but she could see that I could barely stand up and didn't like the idea of talking anymore to someone who could no longer handle their alcohol. I couldn't pull a Hemingway and handle my alcohol. I ended up puking in the barbeque grill, hearing those standing by being repulsed by it. And, there was a pool nearby surrounded by a large fence. So, I took off all my clothes and climbed the fence and went swimming. The next morning I went back to find my underwear, and I had to drive back to my small hometown five hours north in time for work. I called them and told them I would be a little late. It wasn't pleasant driving back with a brutal hangover and going to work looking like I had been in an all night slug fest with the bottle.

After his college football days were over, Huxley still liked to drink but not as much, and I had given up drinking completely. I said to him, "Alcohol kills brain cells." And he said, "Only the bad ones." One night I talked him in to drinking some non-alcoholic beer with me, and he reluctantly said okay. He went and bought a case of it, and he had an annoyed look on his face the whole time. He didn't like it, and he said, "This is just like drinking water."

I like non-alcoholic beer, and I still drink it today. Tonight when I got carded by the police officer who made me show the cashier my ID, it was for some non-alcoholic beer. I have no idea why they card for non-alcoholic beer. I said that one time to a cashier, and he said it was because non-alcoholic beer still has a tiny bit of alcohol in it. I said to him, "Well, this Heineken has none, see O.O%." I love the taste of beer, and it also reminds me of Huxley. Huxley use to say, "Nothing tastes better than pizza and beer.", and when he was in college he took me to a pizza place there in LA where we drank beer and ate a lot of pizza. Huxley use to say, "Pizza and beer compliment one another. That's why they taste so good together." And, he is right. The contrast between each of their taste makes each of their taste even more distinctive. Huxley and I we were very different from one another.

Not too long ago I made a trip to Los Angeles just to go to that pizza place Huxley and I went to and ordered pizza and beer, and I sat there alone eating pizza and drinking beer, thinking about Huxley. I had a real beer for the memory, but now I don't drink. I love the taste of beer, but I hate alcohol. The times I have been most productive is when I wasn't drinking. Some old friends still try to get me to drink with them, and I keep saying no thanks. And, it is difficult to be friends with drinkers because I don't drink. I have seen what too much drinking has done to some people, and it is sad. Huxley use to say that alcohol just makes people be who they really are. This is true, but it can also make some people do stupid things. It has been many years now since Huxley was killed by a drunk driver, and every day I deeply miss him.

"Digging a Dream"

"Nice goosh there, Booga Booga," I said.

"Don't be doggin on me, Wendy," said Trucky.

"I'm not, I'm serious, that's a nice hole you dug up there next to the fence," I said.

"I got inspired by Peter Gabriel's song 'Digging in the Dirt'," said Trucky.

"Ya, that's a great song," I said.

"I know it, I know it, I know it." said Trucky.

"Hey, why don't you ever use the doghouse I built you?" I asked.

"Why don't you use it? You sleep out here, and I'll sleep in your bed," said Trucky.

"Here's your dog food," I said as I put some dry dog food in his bowl alongside his bowl full of water next to his bright blue doghouse.

"You eat it. Momma, fix me a hot dog and corn beef sandwich. I also want a chicken fried, salad, soup sandwich," ordered Trucky.

"Is that a list of things or just one thing?" I asked.

"Don't be doggin on me, Wendy," said Trucky.

"So, do you still believe in Madoogaism?" I asked.

"Yes, I do," quickly stated Trucky with conviction.

"Any new visions today?" I inquired.

"Yes, I was visited by the prophet Badooga. He said that Madooga says that I need to be set free in order to help spread the word of Madooga. You know, make it more ubiquitous," said Trucky.

"So, that's why you were digging the hole next to the fence," I said.

"You are smarter than I thought. I thought you were just completely dumb because you are a human," said Trucky.

"So what is the word of Madooga, and can you explain to me again who Madooga is?" I asked.

"Madooga is a big rottweiler whom I worship. Badooga is a Saint Bernard that tells me what Madooga says," said Trucky.

"Why can't you just talk directly to Madooga?" I asked.

"Badooga needed a job, and Madooga was kind enough to give him one," said Trucky.

"So what is the word of Madooga that you are supposed to spread?" I asked.

"I don't know all of it. I'm supposed to be told more when I'm free. Also, there is the book of Madooga, but I haven't read it yet. I've only heard some of it by Badooga. What I do know is that dogs are supposed to rule the planet because we would do a better job at it than humans. And, humans can help by serving us. We will bring peace on earth!" said Trucky.

"Peace on earth is a great dream. That's my dream too. Why dogs though? If dogs are so intelligent, then why haven't they already ruled over humans?" I asked.

"Well, it took a while for dogs to evolve, but while humans stopped evolving dogs kept evolving and still are," said Trucky.

"So, you really want to be free?" I asked.

"Yes, of course, but feed me a hearty meal first with a large glass of hot chocolate and let me sleep in your bed before I head on out in the morning. This winter night won't be accommodating out here in the cold backyard," said Trucky.

"No, if you really want to be free then I'll open the backyard gate, and you can leave now," I said.

"Okay!" said Trucky.

So, I went over and opened the gate and stood back and motioned for Trucky to go through it. However, Trucky, a big, strong, white huskey, just stood there restlessly motionless and stared at the gate and then curiously glanced at me. Trucky stood there for about five minutes and still didn't move, looking suddenly sad and forlorn. Finally, I asked, "What's wrong? Did you change your mind?"

"If I leave, would you miss me?" asked Trucky.

"Of course. You should know that," I said.

"But if I leave, then you won't have a watch dog," said Trucky.

"I'll get a new dog," I said.

"How could you just replace me like that?" asked Trucky.

"It's your choice to leave, so I don't think it would be unethical to get a new dog," I said.

"It's not this fence that keeps me enslaved. It's the psychological barrier that you created in my psyche. I guess I'll just stay here in the backyard and just sit and dream," said Trucky.

"You can't fool me; you're a big strong dog that fears no one. I can even see you being the leader of a wolf pack somewhere. Why can't you just be honest and admit you don't want to leave because you'd miss me?" I asked.

"Yea, your right. I guess humans are smarter than I thought. But, don't be doggin on me, Wendy," said Trucky.

"Tough Guy"

Charlie woke up again with blood on his designer shirt, and again he didn't know how it got there. It wasn't his blood, but he staggered to the mirror to check his refection to make sure. He was very tall, muscular and looked Mediterranean with long curly black hair. He thought of himself as a beautiful pugnacious man who liked to beat up what he called "tough guys." He didn't like tough guys because he didn't think they were beautiful like him, and not just in appearance, but in many other ways too, so he thought they were jealous of him. He also didn't like them because he thought they were bullies and needed to be taught a lesson.

The night he met Laura in a bar in Austin was just another night where he was wearing makeup and earrings and looking in bars for what he considered tough guys to fight. It was fitting that the song, "Rainy Day Women #12 & 35" by Bob Dylan was playing in the bar at the time because Charlie was about to throw a hefty insult at a big, loud cowboy when he noticed a girl there in the corner by herself which interrupted his mean mission by turning his attention toward her. Instead of fighting, he now wanted love. The girl was Laura, and she was a small, petite blonde. Only a beautiful woman could make Charlie forget about himself. He approached her and put his arm around her and said, "Damn, you're hot!" She was captivated by his forwardness and him, and so they became a couple. While they were together, he temporarily forgot about his pastime of picking fights in bars. She was a somewhat timid music teacher at a junior high school, and he liked trying to bring her out of her shell. She told him that she had never been with a real man before like him. He would use his hands to eat food like salad and even cottage cheese, and she would holler, "That's my baby!" He also impressed her because he was an erudite with two degrees in philosophy and often quoted different philosophers, so she thought he was an intellectual but wondered why he slaved away in a job he didn't seem to care for which was construction and didn't use his degrees. When she asked him, "Why not teach philosophy at a college?", he replied, "I don't want to sell out."

He adored her, but after some time she left him for a poet. She lived only a couple miles away from him, but she sent him a dear john email; and after he read it he fell to the floor and couldn't even flinch. After lying on the floor curled up in a fetus position for three days, he managed to somehow call his boss who came over and took him to a hospital. He spent two months in a mental hospital in which time he worked on an eloquent long hand-written letter to Laura. He wanted his letter to be as fine a letter that Oscar Wilde wrote to Lord Alfred Douglas when Oscar Wilde was in prison. When Charlie got out, he sent her the letter in the mail, and in the letter he asked her to meet him at a specific time in the bar where they first met. He went there hoping to see her, but she never showed up. She had left him for a poet that he had seen before read at a coffee shop that he and Laura liked to go to sometimes, and he didn't understand how she could leave him for a guy who was even smaller than her; also Charlie thought the guy was ugly which reinforced his belief that the war between the beautiful and the ugly was getting worse which a lot of people wouldn't admit. Plus, he thought it wasn't fair that he couldn't beat up the guy because he thought it wasn't right for him to beat up a wimp, so instead he stole the guy's car and wrecked it and then set it on fire.

The next day after that Charlie went back to his construction job. Nobody at work asked him where he had been. His boss knew that Charlie was a troubled man, so he figured that he'd cut him some slack but only for just a little a while because he also didn't want to show favoritism. He was aware of Charlie's long criminal record and had rescued him many times and was tired of it, but he had to keep an eye on his son because he knew his son was too much like himself.

"Too Much Ingenuity"

It was supper time, and Bernard and his dad were busy gobbling up their food. Though never mentioned, they were competing against one another to see who could eat the most and the fastest. They both had curly black hair and were tall but Bernard's dad was taller than Bernard. And, Bernard's father almost always won the eating contest.

After Bernard's father looked up and saw he had won the eating contest again, he looked over at Bernard and said, "Son, I'm a little concerned that you stay in your room too much and play video games. I think you should take up some kind of physical activity sport. I think you should shoot baskets after school. It's time you start acting like a man."

So, Bernard found as many laundry baskets as he could and would shoot them with his BB gun in the backyard, and since they lived outside of town, there were no next-door neighbors to notice. His favorite type of baskets to shoot were Easter baskets; thus he dug up the old Easter baskets that he had when he was a kid in his dad's storage room out in the garage. He was having fun, but his dad came home from work and went in the backyard and was shocked to see Bernard shooting baskets. He yelled at Bernard, "You idiot! When I said you should shoot baskets, I meant basketballs." He believed Bernard didn't have too much ingenuity, but he couldn't imagine how Bernard could misunderstand him past absurdity.

So, Barnard began putting different balls in laundry baskets and shooting them with his BB gun. Again, Bernard's father went out in the backyard and saw what Bernard was doing and was dumbfounded. He yelled at Bernard again, "You idiot! I was talking about the ball that is used in a game of basketball. You know the kind of ball where you dribble and try and put through the hoop. That's the kind of ball I was talking about."

So, Bernard went to the town park after school where there was a pick-up game of basketball that was happening. He hid behind some trees and observed the game from a distance, and when Freddy Musterberg shot a jump shot, Bernard stepped in the clear and with his BB gun shot the basketball in mid-air. The boys playing basketball were at first bewildered and frightened but soon became angry that Bernard with his BB gun shot their basketball which made it flat. That ruined the game, and they chased Bernard who was able to get away.

Later that evening though, the police came to Bernard's house. Bernard was in his room, but he could hear his dad talking to the police about what happened in the living room. Bernard figured he would be arrested. Bernard's dad went to Bernard's room and said to Bernard, "Good job, son. You finally got it right!"

"Never Underestimate a Stranger"

It was a dark night in the city, and I decided to walk to the store. Like usual, I took my mask and would pull it up whenever I passed a stranger. That night there was nobody on the streets, except for one person who seemed to be following me. At first, I just thought it was someone walking in my direction, but I noticed when I sped up, the stranger would too. The stranger seemed to walk at the same pace as me. And, when I stopped, the stranger also stopped. I dismissed it as someone just trying to mess with me and kept walking. Although, it was starting to irritate me. The stranger's big physique would probably appear to be formidable to a lot of people, but I wasn't intimidated because I was also a big man. So, I stopped again and turned around and looked in the stranger's direction. The stranger also stopped and just stood there in the middle of the empty street. I began walking toward the stranger, and the stranger began walking toward me. My heart began pounding. I was getting more perturbed as I walked towards the stranger and pulled up my mask over my nose and mouth. I confronted the stranger but stood at least six feet away from him because of social distancing and said to him, "Why are you following me?"

"I'm not following you. I'm just going to the store," said the stranger who was also wearing a mask.

"I'm not going to the store," I said even though I was.

"Don't lie. You really think you can lie to yourself? You need to stop running away from yourself," said the stranger.

"Who are you?" I asked.

"I'm you," said the stranger.

"What? Ya, right. I don't have time for games. Please stop following me, or I'll call the police," I said.

"I'll stop following you if you stop running from yourself," said the stranger.

I couldn't see the stranger's face because of his mask, the dark night, and he stood at least six feet away from me; however, I thought he was joking or was a homeless man who really just wanted some money or a place to stay which was common. I also knew the town was full of weirdos and thought it may have been just a guy on some drug trip. One night I was approached by guy who clearly was on a drug trip. He was in a parking lot and yelling, and then he approached me and asked, "What kind of questions are you asking?" I didn't answer and just kept walking. Yes, I had seen some strange things before in this town. One lady was shopping and singing church songs and dancing in the isles in a grocery store last summer. Everyone in the store just ignored her, like that stuff is just normal. I grew up in a small town, and I had never seen anything unusual like that in a grocery store there. I had long hair and a beard, and she went up to me and yelled, "Thank you Jesus for my deliverance!" Although, perhaps she really meant it and wasn't on drugs. However, I played along with what the stranger who said he was me and demanded, "If you really are me like you say, then what do you want from me?"

"I only want you to stop running from yourself," said the stranger.

"How am I running from myself? I'm just going to the store. You were the one following me," I said.

"You have been given a gift and need to use it, but you haven't used it like you should," said the stranger.

"What gift?" I asked.

"You know what I'm talking about. You need to get serious about your gift," said the stranger.

"Okay, I will. Now, please go away, or I'll call the police on my cell phone right now," I said. I didn't know what he meant by gift, but I acted like I understood to get him to leave.

"Okay, go use your gift. With your gift, you can do a lot of good for people," he said. And, with those words the stranger turned around and walked away in the night.

I hurried to the store and bought my things and walked back. On the way back, I didn't see the stranger or anyone. But, I kept thinking about what the stranger said. I knew the stranger was crazy, but for some reason I kept wondering what he meant. I didn't believe the stranger was me, but after some thought I realized that what he said was true. And after all, I couldn't see his face, so perhaps he really was me. I didn't believe in surreal experiences, but perhaps this was an exception. Maybe, the stranger really was me. Although, perhaps, I just imagined the whole thing in my mind. I wasn't sure who the stranger was that I met. After that experience though, I didn't secretly criticize people anymore who would tell me about their mystical experiences. Nevertheless, I believe what the stranger said was true. I had been running from myself and not using my gift. So, I stopped making excuses, and I sat down and began writing.

"Don't Bug Me"

From the outside, Cliff looked like he had a lot going for him. He was a comely tall, sleek young man with short curly black hair and glasses and considered intelligent with a good job as an insurance agent. Little did anyone know except for his friend Bill that Cliff had a problem with paranoia because he was able to hide it well. At night around 3 a.m., Cliff would usually wake up in his apartment and start imagining bugs crawling up through the cracks in the walls from the apartment below. He had heard from Bill that Simon who lived below him in the apartment complex had cancer, and Cliff imagined that the bugs that crawled up through the cracks were carrying Simon's cancer. He didn't even know what type of cancer Simon had because Bill hadn't mentioned that detail.

So, he would start panicking about 3 a.m. that the cancer bugs were coming into his apartment. He would jump out of bed and turn on the lights and look all around for bugs, but he almost never saw any bugs, except for an occasional cricket hiding in the corner. He figured that they must run for cover when he turned the light on. He was afraid that when he was asleep the bugs would bite him and infect him with the cancer. He even developed a sore on his leg that he thought may be a bug bite that he repeatedly doctored and examined to try and figure out if it was a bug bite.

He thought about going downstairs and talking to Simon below to see if it really was true that Simon had cancer. He thought that perhaps Bill made it up in order to make him paranoid. That was another dilemma he had. He was paranoid that his friend Bill would purposely tell him things to cause him to worry. He wasn't sure about it though, so he didn't want to accuse Bill of it. It was just another thing that Cliff worried about.

Eventually, he decided to do something about it. He went downstairs to talk to his downstairs neighbor Simon who was on the first floor. Simon was an older man in his sixties with thick wavy gray hair who spent his days sitting outside his apartment smoking cigarettes. He tried to talk to anyone whom he could spot walk nearby. He often tried to talk to Cliff, but when Cliff would come downstairs and see Simon sitting there, Cliff acted like he was in a hurry and had no time to talk. He didn't want to be bugged by Simon. He talked to Simon a few times, but he didn't like talking to Simon because Simon talked too much. However, Cliff now felt bad for Simon because he thought Simon was probably sick, and he also now felt guilty for all those times he tried to avoid talking to Simon. So, Simon was surprised when Cliff went downstairs one morning and stopped to talk to him.

"Good morning, Simon! Couldn't ask for a nicer day!" said Cliff.

"It's a beautiful day! Would you like some coffee?" asked Simon.

"No thank you," said Cliff.

"What can I do for you this morning?" asked Simon.

"I've been worrying about you. I heard that you weren't feeling well," said Cliff.

"Who told you that?" I feel fine," said Simon.

"Oh, well, I'd rather not say. So, you're not sick?" asked Cliff.

"No. Hey, do you want to come over for some soup for lunch?" asked Simon.

"No thank you. I got to get going. Take care," said Cliff.

"You too," said Simon.

Cliff went back up to his apartment and was relieved that Simon didn't have cancer, but he was also now angry at Bill for telling him that. So, he picked up the phone and called Bill.

"Hello," answered Bill. Bill was a tall, muscular athletic young man with long blonde hair who was arrogant and a personal fitness trainer mostly in order to pick up women.

"Hey, Bill, why did you tell me that Simon had cancer? He said he was fine. I just spoke to him," said Cliff.

"I didn't tell you that. You must have imagined it like the bugs," said Bill.

"I know what you told me." said Cliff. "I'm paranoid but not stupid. I'm glad Simon is okay and that I don't have to worry about it anymore. But, my paranoia was right about you. You need to stop bugging me," said Cliff, and then he hung up the phone.

"The Power of Kindness"

Rex used Kirby like a broken toy that still gave him pleasure. Rex told Terrence that Kirby ejaculated on Terrence's pillow. Terrene told me about it in the cafeteria. He was very upset about it because he believed what Rex told him. He said that Rex told him that just as he entered his dorm room, he saw Kirby ejaculate on Terrence's pillow. I told Terrence not to believe Rex, but Terrence said it looked like he did. Later though, Terrence washed his pillow in the sink and saw the soap suds appear and knew it was soap. Rex had put white liquid soap on Terrence's pillow. And there were other unkindly things Rex did to Kirby. One time, Rex and another guy forced Kirby to kiss another guy that Rex and his friends also liked to pick on. Another time, he had Kirby take off his shirt and greased him up and had him wrestle another guy in the hallway who was also shirtless and greased up by some of Rex's friends. Even though Rex tortured Kirby, Kirby still wanted to hang-out with Rex when he could. To Kirby, Rex represented the educated upper class that Kirby wished he was part of. And, it was easy to tell the difference by their appearance: Kirby was tall, rotund, with long black hair, and he wore old tennis shoes, blue jeans, and heavy metal t-shirts; and Rex was a tall, strong short red-headed preppy guy.

So, I felt sorry for Kirby and wanted to help him. Thus, when he'd call and want to hang out, I'd usually go pick him up. He wasn't a college student but liked to hang out with us college guys even though he didn't belong there. The college was an expensive private school, so there were a lot of rich, spoiled preppies there; and Kirby was far from that. He liked his heavy metal music, and he was from a poor, broken family. His parents had mostly just ignored him. I had met him through Terrence who worked with Kirby at Burger King. Kirby liked to make people laugh by telling jokes, but sometimes he'd go way too far with it, especially if he was on one of his drug trips. He was fired from Burger King because one time a customer had a seizure, and Kirby yelled, "Rape her." Nobody thought it was funny.

Even though Kirby apologized and said it was because he was tripping, it didn't matter and only made it worse. Since he had confessed to being on drugs while at work, that was another reason for him to be fired. He couldn't get his job back and couldn't find another job after that. Kirby had a morbid sense of humor and really didn't mean what he blurted out and really did feel bad about what he had yelled.

And, Kirby's biggest problem was he had severe mental problems and had been in and out of mental institutions, and he abusing his medications didn't help. Lithium was his favorite. He had said one time he was very high and jumped someone's fence and began riding their horse. They called the police. Kirby said he jumped on the horse because he was hallucinating that the police were chasing him; however, since he did jump on the horse, the police really did end up chasing him.

One day, Kirby called and wanted to hang out, and so I picked him up.

"Hey, Kirby, how's it going?" I asked as Kirby got into my car.

"Pretty good. We got a new roommate named Sam, and he has been great. He cooks and cleans. He cleaned up the whole house, got rid of all the pestilence," said Kirby with excitement in his voice.

"That's great. Sounds like a nice guy," I said.

"Ya, he is. He also has lung cancer, but he is really positive and has been a great help," said Kirby.

"That's great. Glad you have a new roommate and friend," I said.

"I found God," said Kirby.

"What? You found God? Really?" I asked. I was startled by his sudden declaration.

"Yes. Really," said Kirby.

"That's great! Good for you! How did this come about?" I asked.

"Sam is God," said Kirby.

"What?" I asked.

"You heard me. Sam is God," said Kirby.

"He's not God," I said.

"Okay," said Kirby.

We drove around the city awhile and went and visited different friends that I had, and each place we went to they didn't like me bringing Kirby along. They would ask to speak to me outside and tell me to take Kirby and leave and not to bring him back. I thought that my most liberal friends would not turn him away, but they did too. Nobody wanted to be around Kirby except Rex and his friends to pick on him and also some guys who wanted Kirby to hook them up with drugs. I once took Kirby to one of my juggling club meetings, and one girl was there for the first time but never went back. Later, she said it was because Kirby scared her.

After driving around and trying to visit people, we went back to my apartment. There, Kirby started fighting in the air what he called were demons. He then could see I was uncomfortable about him acting like that and said to me, "You better take me home."

I said, "Okay."

"Will you write about me?" he asked.

"Yes, Kirby. I'll write about you," I said.

"A Nose for Music"

I didn't like the guy, so this is what I did. I decided to shrink myself and went into his ear and played on his ear drum which gave him a horrible headache. The man kept hearing a banging in his ear, and when he went to the doctor, the doctor couldn't see anything wrong with it. That was because I made sure and left his ear before his visit to the doctor. So, this went on for a while, and the man about went insane. After a while, I went up his nose and began to play his nose hairs like a harp which tickled his nose, and the man kept itching it and sneezing. Again, the man went to see his doctor, but the doctor couldn't find anything wrong with the man. The doctor told the man that he thought it was just psychological and referred the man to a shrink. So, the man went to a shrink who told the man that his symptoms were from childhood trauma, like the man was picked last during gym class or something dumb like that, and the shrink put the man on some medication. Oh ya, the guy's father called him a chump one time. I must confess though that I began to feel sorry for the man and stopped the foolishness, and the man's symptoms went away. He was even able to get off the medication and stopped being played by a shrink. Being able to shrink myself whenever I want to has given me a lot of power, and I need to be careful about abusing it. However, that man I told you about deserved it, and I knew when to stop it. Eventually though, I stopped using my power to shrink because I found a greater power, words.

"Time for Class"

When I was a student at Rice University in Houston, Texas, different people would fight over who would get to hang out with me. One person was a few years older than me. His name was Bill, and he was a handsome short, thin guy with curly black hair, black eyes and olive skin. He came from a very wealthy family in Greenwich, Connecticut; although, he was ashamed of it and didn't want people to know it. So, he would wear haggard clothes and drive an old beat-up pick-up truck.

I was from a poor family and was there on an academic scholarship, but I wished I was rich; so I liked being around rich people. I read books about rich characters by writers like F. Scott Fitzgerald and Edith Wharton. I had also chosen Rice University since Howard Hughes went there. And, different rich people there liked having me around because they knew that I was a gifted student and liked giving me things.

Even though Bill dressed like a transient and didn't shower much, he would buy fancy clothes but wouldn't wear them. He'd put them in his closet for a while and then give them to me. One time, he put all his posh clothes in a big bag and took it to my apartment and dropped it on the floor and said, "Here Mickey, this is for you!" Thus, there I was, a poor kid, going to class in designer clothing worth thousands. Just as Bill was hiding that he was rich, I was hiding that I was poor. Bill wanted to be a rebel, and I wanted to fit in.

And, Bill gave me a lot of things, many music CDs and would come to my apartment door with food to give me. I remember him banging on my door and yelling, "Mickey, I know you're in there! I bought your favorite pizza for you!" And, when I visited his home in Greenwich, Connecticut, it was like a palace, and his dad gave us a lot of spending cash just to go run around Manhattan which we did and spent all of it in two days.

My girlfriend Tammy at the time in college didn't like Bill and had a rule that he wasn't allowed in her apartment, so I took him over there one night because I resented that she constantly complained about him; and he rolled around on her floor and giggled which made her livid. Before that one time, she was complaining about Bill and said, "I know 100% that he's gay and is obsessed with you."

"No, Bill is not gay. Besides, he'd still be my friend even if he was," I said.

One night, Bill called me up and wanted to meet me in front of the Rice Student Center. I said okay and went there that night. My apartment was close to campus, so I didn't have to walk far. When I got there, I could tell Bill had been crying.

"Hey Bill, how's it going?" I asked.

"Not good, Mickey. Cindy left me for Vince. I should had seen it coming," lamented Bill.

"Sorry to hear that, Bill," I said.

"I've been seeing demons, and I can't get them to go away. Will you hold me and tell me you love me, Mickey?" asked Bill.

"What? Why?" I asked.

"I need your help, and you're the only friend I have," said Bill.

"Okay," I said. So, I held him and told him that I loved him, but I felt very awkward about it. I wasn't really there even though I was there, not because I didn't want to help. I felt bad for him, but I didn't know what I could do except listen and watch him begin to start sobbing.

When Cindy and Bill were together, Cindy would call me on the phone to complain about Bill when she was having problems with him. It was mostly when Bill stopped taking his medication. Bill had been in counseling and on medication since he was a child, but he had never talked about it to me. I knew this because Cindy had told me. With me, he usually acted like everything was fine and like a tough guy who liked to talk guy stuff. We would go to a park and throw the football around and talk football. So, I was surprised to see him like that in front of the Rice Student Center that night, but I shouldn't have expected him to hide that from me as something he bought for me.

"The Cool Bear in the Dumpster"

One night, when I was in graduate school, I went to throw some trash away in the dumpster in the parking lot of the apartment complex where I lived. I opened the dumpster door and was shocked to see a big man in the dumpster. I yelled, "What are you doing in here?"

The man growled, "Looking for something."

The man's name was Toby, and he also lived in the same apartment complex as me. That night, he looked like a busy bear in the dumpster with a flashlight looking for food in the garbage, but it wasn't food that he was searching for. Being curious, I didn't just walk off but waited around to see what he had to say because I knew he loved to talk. He said he was ready to get out, so I helped him out of the dumpster. Toby was a tall, big man with black hair that he wore in a pompadour. He smelled of garbage as we stood in the parking lot for a while as if it was perfectly normal to find someone in a dumpster to chat with, and he had told me that the reason he had climbed into the dumpster was because he threw away his porn in that dumpster earlier that morning but had changed his mind about it that night and tried to recover it.

Toby was very religious which was probably one reason he was so conflicted at times by his sex addiction. One minute he'd be talking about the church which he attended regularly and how he had overcome his licentiousness, and then the next minute he'd be talking about his online sex hook-up club he belonged to which he consistently paid monthly dues to. From what he said, members of this club like him were into a lot of strange sexual fetishes. One time, he showed me a letter from a woman who said she couldn't sleep with him because he looked like her brother.

Toby was in the same graduate school program as me, but I first met him when he had accused me of hitting his motorcycle in the parking lot. He saw blue paint on his damaged motorcycle and thought it must had been from my blue car. He approached me and demanded that I pay for the damage. I told him that it wasn't from my car and showed him I didn't have a scratch on my car, so he dropped it and we began talking.

In classes, Toby liked to talk a lot, and I kept silent and only spoke when I had something important to say. He often would say something controversial which helped make him unpopular. On the first day of one class, he kept raising his hand, and the professor told him to put his hand down.

Toby wasn't well liked out of the classroom too. Some football players glued pennies on the bottom of his front door one time because he had called them dumb. And, there were those who didn't think it was cool that Toby dressed like the Fonz because he was the president of a fan club for the old TV show *Happy Days*. He was obsessed with other old TV shows too. Being anachronistic, he often talked about how great American morals were in the 1950s and early 1960s. Though his obsession with *Happy Days* was probably innocuous, it caused him ridicule.

Toby's outdated style didn't seem to help him with girls, and he had trouble talking to them. One time, a tall, thin redheaded girl named Lisa approached me and was crying and told me that Toby had told her that I said she was a bitch. I explained to her that it wasn't true, and then I asked Toby why he told her that. He said, "Well, I'm basically socially screwed up."

However, Toby tried to make it up to me. He had a knack for making prank calls and pretending to be another person. So, I gave him the phone number of a petite blonde girl named Rhonda who gave me her phone number because she liked me, and he called her and pretended to be another guy. He had her going for a while, but then I think she caught on and pretended to go along with it. However, she also somehow figured out it was Toby. So, when I saw her again, she asked, "Did you give Toby my phone number?"

"Yes. Sorry about that. It was just a joke," I said.

"That's okay," she said.

"Glad you're cool with it. I'll tell Toby," I said.

"I'm not cool with Toby. I reported him to campus police," she said.

Though Rhonda never said it, her eyes confirmed my intuition that it was really me she was angry at about it and not Toby because she wanted to date me.

And, by Toby telling Lisa the truth, Toby proved to me that he could not be trusted. He threw away whatever potential friendship we had and tried to recover it with charm like the prank call.

However, that's okay. We remained cordial. And though we lost touch after graduate school, I wish Toby well wherever he is now and hope he stays out of the dumpster.

"Tug-of-War"

Wesley loved sports, and he also loved the arts. His dad fostered his love of sports while his mother nurtured his love of the arts. His father never got a chance to coach him because Wesley was too good at sports, so they made a rule just because of him that no father was allowed to coach his son. Wesley (a tall, strong, lanky black-haired boy) dominated in many sports and was always the leader of whatever sport or team he was on. On the other hand, his mother had him taking piano lessons, be in the school choir, and also had him sing at family gatherings. When he got to high school, Wesley made show choir, and he was also the starting varsity quarterback. It got to the point though were Wesley felt conflicted because he was being pulled in two different directions.

The football coach, Coach Manton, a tall, bulky middle-aged man with spiked blond hair in a crew cut, was his mentor, but so was his show choir teacher, Mr. Trench, also a middle-aged man but with black hair, taller than Coach Manton but quite thinner. These men were vastly different from one another. Coach Manton believed that sports were necessary for boys to play in order to learn how to become men. And, Mr. Trench believed that the arts were necessary for boys to embrace in order to become men. Coach Manton said to Wesley at practice one day, "You need to quit show choir because it interferes with you being the quarterback and all your other sports. Also, how do you think it looks to others that you are in show choir? You are the leader of the team and need to show strength and not be involved in something so less masculine. You are a great athlete and great quarterback. You have been given a rare gift and need to focus on it." However, Mr. Trench told Wesley in class one day, "You need to quit football and all the other sports and only focus on show choir. You have a rare gift and need to focus on it."

And one time, the two men got into a shouting match which led to a fight in the school parking lot over Wesley. Each thought the other was a bad influence on Wesley. Coach Manton didn't like Wesley being late for practice because of show choir practice, so he went to Mr. Trench's office to speak to him about it and went in without knocking first.

"Wesley was late again to practice because of show choir. You need to stop having long rehearsals or let Wesley leave early," said Coach Manton as he shut the door behind him.

"Hello, Coach Manton. It wouldn't be fair to the others or the boy to allow Wesley to leave early. We also have a big show coming up, and Wesley has a lead part which he needs to learn," said Mr. Trench.

"Well, we got a big playoff game coming up, and we are learning some new plays for the game that the other team hasn't seen before. Also, how do you think it looks to the team when their quarterback shows up late time and time again," said Coach Manton.

"That's not my concern. I have to teach my class the way I think is best. Now, if you excuse me, I got a lot of work to do," said Mr. Trench.

"I can't expect someone like you to understand what you are doing to the boy," said Coach Manton.

"What do you mean, someone like me?" asked Mr. Trench.

"You probably never played a sport before. So, you wouldn't know what it takes," said Coach Manton.

"I played sports in high school. I was a quarterback too. I know how demanding it can be," said Mr. Trench.

"You? That's hard to believe," said Coach Manton.

"Like I said, I got a lot of work to do. Hey look, I'm not gonna let you bully me. To be honest, I don't think you are a good example for Wesley. He has a gift and needs to use it," said Mr. Trench.

"Ya, he is a great athlete and great quarterback and needs to use it. You may have been a quarterback at one time, but you don't seem to understand. The world needs a boy like Wesley to become a great man and help lead this country. We need men who can lead and fight. We need great quarterbacks and great athletes. This country wasn't built by effeminate men like yourself. This country wasn't built by the arts. We need warriors," said Coach Manton.

"The arts teach creativity, emotional intelligence, empathy, and many other things you know nothing about. Football, and any sport, is only a game," said Mr. Trench.

"It's not just a game, and you know it. I don't know what happened to you, but I won't let you turn the boy into a beta male," said Coach Manton.

"Please leave! Get out!" yelled Mr. Trench.

"Don't yell at me! Why don't we take this conversation outside and settle this like real men!" hollered Coach Manton back even louder.

So, the two men stormed out of Mr. Trench's office and marched down the hallway and out into the parking lot and kept shouting at each other which turned into a fist fight. Students quickly found out about it, and there became a spectacle. Mr. Trench could fight which surprised Coach Manton. Coach Manton just thought he could knock Mr. Trench out with one swing, but it didn't go that way. The fight went on for several minutes, and each man was out of shape. So, eventually, both men could barely swing. Wesley didn't see it but heard about the fight. Though he was never told, Wesley could sense that the men were fighting over him.

The next year, Wesley chose football over show choir, but he never lost his love for beauty.

"A Dirt Road to Freedom"

"It's not the size of the dog in the fight. It's the size of the fight within the dog." - Mark Twain

In the small town of Pinewood, Arizona, there lived a pious couple with their four sons in a humble home on a cinder road. The fourth child's name was Scott who was a small, wiry kid with curly blond hair and very tough who fought a lot and had never lost a fight, but he thought his dad Carl was somewhat weak. He wished his dad was more like his next-door neighbor Mr. Childress whom Scott lionized because Mr. Childress was a big, strong man with blond hair that was buzzed like a soldier. He was a veteran who had fought in combat. Carl was a small quiet man with curly blond hair like his son and an accountant who had never fought in a war or had been in the military. Scott thought his dad acted too gentlemanly and also knew when he grew up he would become a professional football player or a marine like Mr. Childress and definitely not an accountant like his dad. Scott knew his dad was a good man, but he also saw that on the playground the outcome of battles weren't determined by who was the most virtuous kid, but won by the toughest which often was the biggest, except in his case.

He had beaten up kids a lot bigger than himself.

Carl never resented Mr. Childress, and Mr. Childress was never condescending toward Carl. Carl just figured it was normal for the youngest son to rebel against his father. He had remembered how rebellious his youngest brother was toward his father. Carl's youngest brother Greg had talked back and even almost got into physical altercations with his dad. That's not how it was though with Scott and his dad. Scott didn't talk back to Carl. No, that wasn't the problem. The problem was he didn't want to talk at all with his dad and would usually only give his dad yes or no answers. Carl would say, "How was school today, son?" And, Scott would answer, "Fine." Carl would try and get more information out of Scott, but Scott was stubborn and wouldn't talk. Carl would ask, "How was practice today, son?" Scott would answer, "Fine." That kind of repetition went on for quite a stretch many nights. Scott was a quarterback in little league football on a team called the Dolphins, and though Carl went to Scott's games and supported him Carl didn't know much about football; but Mr. Childress had been a high school quarterback and would play catch with Scott on the cinder road and talk to him about football.

Carl never had a very good relationship with his father mostly because his father was usually away on business, so Carl never had a dad who taught him how to play sports or be there for him that much. Carl had to figure out a lot of things on his own. Carl had been a studious child who read a lot of books growing up and was a great accountant that made good money to support his family, but he wasn't the macho type that Scott revered and wanted to be like.

One day, Scott and his older brothers and other kids were playing football in a field near their neighborhood, and their family dog Burt whom Scott was close to was running away from the dog catcher nearby. Burt was a big, yellow mongrel and very loyal to the family. The dog catcher Morton had been catching dogs that were not on a leash all over town and then taking them to the dog pound and putting them to sleep. Carl let Burt run around town without a leash like a lot of other dogs because it was a small town and nobody seemed to mind. But, in the last couple of weeks, Morton had caught quite a few dogs, and though people were complaining nobody did anything about it because Morton had a new town ordinance on his side. Plus, Morton was six foot six and weighed two hundred and sixty pounds. The only man bigger than Mr. Childress in town was Morton, and they were friends that grew up together and played high school football together. Morton also looked intimating because his short hair and beard were black.

Morton used a tranquilizer gun to catch the dogs, and Scott saw Morton shoot Burt; and Burt knew that he was being chased and had been hit, so he ran back to the house while Morton, like Ahab after the whale, chased him from behind. Carl was in the front yard when Burt came running up to him. Morton approached Carl and the dog Burt in the front yard. Scott, his brothers, and other kids followed behind and watched. Morton didn't hesitate but walked up to take Burt, but Burt hid behind Carl. Morton said, "Carl, I'm gonna have to take your dog."

"Why?" asked Carl.

"I shot him with a tranquilizer gun, and he'll be going to sleep here pretty soon," said Morton.

"Burt can sleep it off here. You're not taking our dog," said Carl.

"Yes, I am," said Morton.

"No, you're not," said Carl.

Mr. Childress next door noticed the commotion and walked over and saw what was happening and looked at Carl and said, "Carl, you better let him take Burt. There's a new town ordinance about dogs running around without a leash. It wouldn't be fair to others if you didn't let him take Burt," said Mr. Childress.

"The others should have stood up to this nonsense. You can give me a warning, and I'll make sure Burt stays on a leash next time he is about town," said Carl.

"No, I'm taking your dog, stand aside Carl. Don't make me get physical with you," said Morton.

"No, you're not taking our dog. Period. I'll fight you if I have to," said Carl.

Morton realized that Carl wasn't bluffing. He stood there for a while thinking about whether he should make a move or not. Nobody had stood up to him before about this, so this was a new situation for him. Scott was surprised too. He had never seen his dad act like that before. His dad had always been so mild mannered. Morton finally said, "Well, there's no reason fighting over this. I would only end up hurting you. I don't want to hurt you Carl. You're a good man. I'll let it be, but if I see that dog again around town without a leash I'll be using something stronger than a tranquiller gun," said Morton and then walked away.

Scott had never been more proud of his dad at that moment. Scott had thanked his dad that day for standing up to Morton and not letting Morton take their dog. However, he never told him how proud he had been of him. So, years later he told his dad how proud he was of him that day and apologized for not telling him. Carl responded, "Don't worry about it. I knew it. You didn't have to say anything. I hope you also learned that day that a man should only fight when he needs to."

After Morton had walked away that day he shot Burt with the tranquiller gun, Carl had put Burt in the garage, and Burt slept. The family had worried about Burt, but after three days Burt woke up and seemed robust once again and ready to eat and then go outside again to play. However, this time they kept Burt in the backyard, and when they took him around town they kept him on a leash. Morton kept hoping he'd catch Burt about town not on a leash, but it didn't happen. So, one day, Morton snuck into Carl's backyard to try and capture Burt. Burt saw Morton and hid under the porch and was shaking with fear. Fortunately, Carl's wife Grace came home early from work and caught Morton in the backyard and chased him off and told him to never do that again.

Carl still let Burt roam free without a leash outside of town. They'd put him in the back of the truck and take him miles outside of town on dirt roads to run around without a leash. One time, outside of town Morton was driving in his pickup truck, and he was wearing a short sleeve shirt and had his passenger side window rolled down with his arm resting on the bottom of it. And, Burt chased the pick-up truck and then jumped up and bit Morton on the forearm.

"Speaking with the Eyes"

We walked into the restaurant, and the Smith's song "How Soon is Now" was blaring; and I said to Aline, "Ah, the Smiths, one of my favorites." We sat down and ordered and tried to talk, but it was too loud in the place. So, we mostly just looked at one another and spoke to each other with our eyes since there was plenty of light to see. She had hope in her eyes as she stared at me, and I looked away and then looked back and could see the change in her eyes. By I looking away, her eyes and even the rest of her face told me that she understood that I didn't want to be with her. But, she kept still kept hoping and pursuing me. She had been persistent for years, and it was difficult telling her each time that I only wanted to be friends because she was such good person and whom most men would dream of being with. A beautiful, kind, intelligent woman, she was statuesque-looking, tall, with long light-brown hair, and from France, and she had a dream of becoming an American and finding the ideal American guy; and she thought I was the ideal American guy.

She figured that if she became close friends with me then eventually I would want to be more than friends with her. But, it wasn't a film. I should not have hung out with her so much because it made things more difficult for her. We were fascinated with one another because she was European and spoke nine languages, and I was an American; and even though I had multiple degrees I only knew how to speak English like many Americans, except for a little German that I took as a requirement for one of my degrees. I was particularly interested in France, and even though I had never been there I had studied it and had read many of the French writers such as the poets Arthur Rimbaud, Paul Verlaine, and Charles Baudelaire. She would read me their poetry in French; although, I didn't understand French. And, she gave me great advice. We would give each other books to read and discuss them and also watch films together and discuss them. We watched the film *Before Sunrise*.

One might think all those nights we stayed up talking that we would have gotten together, but it never happened. She was certainly physically attractive. Guys were constantly hitting on her, but she was focused on me. I remember going to a watcher park with her, and she wore a bikini. There, after riding a water slide, I went to get a drink, and I noticed an attractive woman that I was checking out; and then I noticed it was Aline and was embarrassed because she could see the look in my eyes that I was attracted to her, so her eyes sparked clearly with excitement.

The last time I spent with her was in her apartment. We were sitting on the couch, and I said that I needed to go. She said, "Please don't go. You're just using me."

I said, "No, I'm not."

She asked, "Why can't you make up your mind about me?"

"I've told you before I would like to just be friends," I said.

"Are you gay?" she asked.

"No," I said.

"Is it because I'm not American?" she said.

"No," I said.

"I always knew you were crazy," she said.

"I'm not crazy," I said.

"Then why won't you love me?" she asked.

"You're a good friend. Why can't a man and woman just be good friends?" I asked.

"Well, why the hell would I be giving you gifts and spending all this time with you? I want us to get somewhere," she said. I didn't say anything. I had learned that most women don't want to hang out with a guy and be friends with them unless they are interested in them romantically. Some women have told me that's not true, but that's what I've noticed.

I got up to leave, and she got up and ran over and blocked the door. I stood there for a while and asked her to please move. She stood there with a determined look in her eyes saying that she was refusing to let me go which seemed to last for a long time, so I went and sat down on the couch until she finally moved away from the door and also went and sat down on the couch. And then, I got up and left.

Not too long after that, she got married. I missed her as a friend, but we still kept in touch once in a while by phone and email, only to say hello. My parents loved her, so they expressed their disappointment to me that she and I never got together. Plus, Aline was rich, and I was poor. I have been asked why she and I never got together. A friend asked me, "Why didn't you and Aline ever get together? What? Do you have a problem with beautiful women?" I answered, "No. You're hilarious. This is probably difficult for you and many people to understand, but the truth is that it just didn't work out." At first, he thought I was just being clever and playful again and still wanted some answers, but then he changed his mind and stayed quiet about it because he saw in my eyes that I had said enough.

"Dry Tears"

On the outside, Marty felt paralyzed. Like a sick Buddhist, Marty wished he would have been able to reach out of himself more at his brother Horace's funeral to express how he felt and get some relief away from his inner turmoil. But, it had been so awkward for him because he usually avoided such situations. He was tall, skinny, and had sleepy yet piercing eyes, and those who did not know him did not know whether he was just sleepy or in deep thought. As usual, Marty was in deep thought.

Marty was an emotional thinker and not an emotional do-er. He had an English degree, but he did not even know how to change a tire; therefore, for him to cry in public was even more of a long shot. Marty could not say much to his profusely grieving mother at the funeral except "He's with God now, and we'll see him again someday" even though he hardly believed it himself. And, it stung him when his mother said to him, "Where's your emotion boy?"

The funeral was in the same church where Horace was married, but it was even a bigger event than the wedding: the mayor of Dallas and the whole police department was present because Horace had been a Dallas policeman. Horace's wife was on meds, but members of her family still had to drag her in through the doors while she was hysterically screaming. Marty had never seen anything like it before. Lots of people were crying; even Marty's father was crying which startled Marty because he had never seen his dad cry before. His dad had taught him the importance of being mentally strong by being an example of it. His dad was tough, and Marty never saw him back down from a fight. Marty was like that too. Being mentally tough was crucial to being a man is what his dad thought. He remembered his dad telling him, "I know you're physically tough, but I worry that you are not mentally tough." He told Marty this when Marty was a teenager, and it always stayed there in the back of Marty's mind.

Marty knew he had to be tough, and he was though he doubted if he really was underneath his bravado.

One of Horace's children, a little boy with black hair, was also bawling at the funeral, and people were passing him around like a hot potato. Someone handed him to Marty, and Marty hugged the little boy and felt sorry for him. Marty could see Horace in Horace's little boy. The little boy's crying reminded Marty of a time when he and Horace were kids and one night the joy bus of the church their family attended left Horace behind at church, and Marty remembered that when the joy bus pulled back into the parking lot, there was Horace standing there, crying.

When Marty was in Dallas to attend the funeral, the song "Where have all the Cowboys?" by Paulo Cole kept playing on the car radio, and as Marty drove his car listening to the song he thought the song to him was about his brother Horace. Marty loved his brother Horace and knew Horace had been a great man and police officer. So, while listening to that song he recalled the story he had heard from another police officer that one time while on duty Horace found a naked homeless man, and, instead of taking the man to jail, Horace, out of his own pocket, bought the man clothes and food. To Marty, the song was about where have the great men gone, and he knew Horace was a great man.

At the funeral, Marty presented the eulogy. He could always perform well under pressure even in a crisis and figured it had something to do with him being left-handed which he had learned from doing research on left-handers. Horace had also been left-handed. Marty read his poem and gave a speech with as much intentional external emotion as necessary to do the job properly. Also, in his speech, he talked about how Horace was tough on him and how he appreciated it. He closed his speech by saying, "Is there an afterlife? Well, I have to believe there is because I want to see my brother again." Marty received praise for his speech and also how he was able to deliver it calmly under the circumstances. However, Marty had guilt because he felt like his speech had some affectation to it. What bothered him was that he was not able to show his emotions, not in the way that was truly how he felt. But, Marty secretly knew himself. He waited until the funeral was over and when he was back at graduate school in Ohio, so that he could go off by himself to weep.

Back at graduate school Marty's pain had reached a zenith and was becoming unbearable. He had worn the poker face for too long. He didn't want to wear the mask anymore. Like many American boys, he had been raised to believe that emotion is a weakness and real men are stoic, especially in public. He practiced the Hemingway code: grace under pressure. He saw this code in his mentors, coaches, teachers, older brothers, father and grandfathers. However, Marty was thinking that perhaps he was too sensitive because he was having a difficult time containing his feelings. So, he began running in the dark hours of night, so nobody would see his pain. And, he also convinced himself that he would somehow escape it by doing physical exercise. He had learned from his dad that the best way to handle most problems is by doing physical exercise.

One night he tried with all his might to run away from it until he fell on the track sobbing and then rolled on his back and began screaming up at the sky as if it was the sky's fault. As a child Marty had learned that God was up above and the devil was down below. Thus, when he was little, he and his female friend across the street tried very hard to dig up the devil in his backyard. They even tried to find the devil in an acorn once after they had no luck digging up the devil. Now, he was looking up at the sky trying to see if God was watching and hearing him. Marty was confused because he could not understand why God would take away his brother, Horace, a great man, and also in such a cruel, senseless way. Horace was killed by a drunk driver when he was coming home from work one night, and he left behind a wife and two children. Marty felt bad that happened to Horace.

The news of Horace's death came as a horrible shock to Marty, but what made it worse was that Marty never worried about Huxley before. Horace was the biggest and strongest in the family. He certainly perfected the Hemingway code. At the time of his death, Horace was twenty-eight-years-old and was six foot three and weighed 280 pounds. But, that was just his physical size. Horace was extremely tough. Marty remembered how Horace would lift weights: Horace would bang his head on the bar before he would squat a heavy weight like 800 pounds. And, to this day, there is an award given in Horace's name called the "Horace Regions Man of Steel" award which is given to the toughest guy on the college team that Horace played for. As a police officer Horace was the first one that the other officers would call if there was a problem that got out of hand. Marty did a ride around with him one time, and Horace kept telling Marty to become a police officer; however, Marty didn't have an interest in it.

So, Marty lied there sobbing and screaming up at the sky that one Ohio night around 2 in the morning. He was on the school's track, and nobody was around. Thus, he felt that the track there was a safe haven for him to grieve at that time. But, to Marty the loss of Horace made everything seem chaotic. Lying there on the ground that night and looking up at the sky, Marty could not see God. Instead, he had a feeling that the earth was falling into the sky and that there was no direction or order to the universe.

The next couple of weeks Marty began pondering even more over what happened to his brother. He realized that death was inevitable and that what happened to his brother made him become more aware of it. Marty remembered reading Saul Bellow's novel *Henderson the Rain King*, and he thought of how Henderson said that truth comes in blows. Marty knew that death is not just a blow that comes and goes--but it remains. He thought that he would never be the same again.

Marty wanted to curse God all the time, but he was too afraid to. He had been taught that God had a mean streak in him and one should not upset him. Perhaps, he thought his feelings came from his puritan ancestors. However, it did not seem fair to Marty that God could upset him but he should remain silent. Although, Marty was afraid of God, and soon he became afraid of almost everything, even the way the trees would branch over him when he went for runs or walks alone at night.

Also, whenever Marty felt pleasure, he would torture himself with guilt. It was a new, uncanny kind of ferocious despair stirring deep within his depth. Chaos was slowly flooding him. Marty had read a lot of Friedrich Nietzsche's books such as *Thus Spoke Zarathustra*, from which Nietzsche said, "One must still have chaos in oneself to be able to give birth to a dancing star," and Marty felt that Nietzsche was calling him but giving "birth to a dancing star" was too painful.

Marty spent many nights talking to Nietzsche based on the books he had read by Nietzsche. He thought Nietzsche was wrong when Nietzsche said that the highest beauty in life was tragedy. Even if it made him stronger (which he highly doubted), he thought no way was it beautiful in any way and definitely not worth it. He understood that one's realization of possible tragedy in one's life made one's joyous moments more intense. However, he thought one should not have a tragedy just so others can have intense joy. And, he thought that one should not experience tragedy in order to experience joy. It also infuriated Marty when people, who remained untouched by tragedy, thought that they were more blessed by God than the ones who endured horrific tragedies. "Could joy exist without tragedy?" he pondered.

Marty had hardy no one to talk to about such questions, and he felt as though everyone seemed like a closed book because they didn't want to cross the line of propriety. He thought that those who cross the line are kicked out of the game and that it was sad. He believed that truth should be spoken instead of written in books about how it is hidden. At times Marty tried to talk to some of his teachers or other students about what happened to Horace, but everyone seemed too uncomfortable or in a hurry to talk about it. Instead, they would give him one liners and split. Marty realized that perhaps they were afraid to talk about death or why God allows tragedy to happen in the lives of good people. Marty speculated that many people also avoided such topics because they did not want to think of their own mortality or be challenged to question their belief systems.

But, there was one professor who talked to him about it. One day after a class Marty waited around to talk to one of his mentors, Dr. Smith. Dr. Smith saw that Marty was still just sitting there in his seat.

"Did you need something?" asked Dr. Smith to Marty.

"No," said Marty.

"Can I ask you something?" asked Dr. Smith.

"Ya, sure," said Marty.

"I'm sorry to hear what happened to your brother. How's your mommy and daddy?" asked Dr. Smith.

"They are okay," said Marty.

"Did you see the connection between what happened to your brother and Stephen Crane's short story "The Open Boat?" asked Dr. Smith.

"Huh, what do you mean?" asked Marty.

"Well, wasn't your brother a big football hero?" asked Dr. Smith.

Marty answered, "He was Honorable Mention in the Big 12 Conference. But, he was the strongest guy on the team. He could bench over 500 pounds, and they still give out an award for the toughest guy on the team in his name." Marty was given a chance to brag about Horace, and he seized the moment.

"Well, in Crane's story, Billie, the Oiler, is the strongest out of the men, and ironically he dies," said Dr. Smith.

"Ya, I see," said Marty.

"What do you know about the drunk driver who killed your brother?" asked Dr. Smith.

"She was a twenty-one-year-old girl," replied Marty.

"Do you see the irony in that? A little girl takes the life of a big, strong man. Do you see the irony?" asked Dr. Smith.

"Ya," said Marty.

"Is your brother's widowed wife pretty?" asked Dr. Smith.

"What?" responded Marty.

"If she is pretty then she might be able to marry again, so your brother's kids will have a daddy," said Dr. Smith.

"I suppose," said Marty.

"So how you doing anyways?" asked Dr. Smith.

"I'm fine. You know trying to stare death in the eyes is terrifying," said Marty.

"Yes. It's the most terrifying. You know, those who love life the most also fear death the most. It's okay to be afraid of death. Funny thing though really, most people want to go to heaven, but they don't want to die," Dr. Smith said and began laughing.

"Ya," Marty said and forced a little smirk.

Marty loved Dr. Smith as his mentor, but he thought that talking to Dr. Smith that day was a strange experience. As Marty left the classroom, he was irritated how Dr. Smith used Huxley's death as an example of Stephen Crane's philosophy in his short story "The Open Boat." However, Marty was also glad that Dr. Smith was talking to him about it.

Marty's relationship with his brother Horace was also a strange one. Growing up Horace was tough on Marty because he thought that Marty being the youngest in the family was spoiled. He wanted to teach Marty how to be tough like him. As a child he once painted Marty in tar from head to toe. It took Marty's mom hours to scrub the tar off while Marty screamed. And when they would play football, Horace would tackle Marty very hard. Marty did not like getting hit so hard and was contemplating giving it up; however, Horace made Marty a crown out of paper and called Marty the Touchdown King. That got Marty excited again, and so Marty went back out to play football with the big boys convinced that he was the Touchdown King and also not knowing that big brother made him the crown in order to cream him some more.

Growing up, Marty was the skinny quarterback, and Horace was the big lineman. Horace liked to pick on Marty all in the name of making him tougher. Horace often would say to Marty, "Quarterbacks are pencil necks. You're just a little pencil neck quarterback." Horace prided himself on being big and would say, "Eat to win."

Back at graduate school in Ohio, Marty continued running and pondering over what happened to Horace. When he first got the news of what happened, he was in bed early in the morning. Campus security came by and woke him up and told him to call home. Marty knew someone probably had died, but Horace was the last person he thought of. He called home, and his mother told him. The first thing Marty did was go running that morning. As he ran he felt like he was under water, and his ears were ringing. The truth of what happened was too shocking, and it came too suddenly. Later, he also thought what Milan Kundera had said was true in his novel *The Unbearable Lightness of Being*. There is no rehearsal in life; we don't even know what our next line will be most of the time.

Whenever Marty speculated on such things, he also often thought of Emily Dickinson's poem: "Tell all the truth but tell it slant--(1263)." And, he wondered who is qualified to tell the truth? However, feeling was a different matter. No matter what the truth really was, his pain was real. After each philosophical battle that Marty had with himself, emotion was the only one left standing. This he knew was real; this he could prove to himself. Emotion was a fact, and yet it was chaotic and a mystery. It was a fact that could not be defined or calculated. It was beyond understanding, and yet it still was there, very real, and in him. Finally, Marty realized this truth and embraced it. Eventually, he stopped trying to run from his pain.

About six months after the funeral, Marty was sitting in a classroom listening to a professor lecture about some depressing novel. Marty was sitting there quietly taking in the lecture and taking notes. Occasionally, he would raise a question that impressed the class. Many of Marty's classmates and teachers always admired the strength that Marty portrayed in many ways on the outside. Marty had the look of the cold, calculated intellectual, but if you watched the nuances of his eyes too carefully every now and then he would look out the window with a sad look searching for his brother Horace.

"The Hidden Stack"

Pinewood, Arizona was a beautiful small town surrounded by mountains that sheltered it from the harsh winters. Growing up there, I was surrounded by my family who looked out for me too. My oldest brother Joe didn't look like a fighter, but he was. He had to be because our family were outsiders, and Joe being the oldest had to help clear a path for his younger brothers. A lot of other kids picked fights with Joe because Joe not only didn't look like a fighter but he was an outsider and a new kid in town. And, my family didn't belong to the main church there which didn't help us fit in either.

Joe was short and overweight and had thick black glasses. He struggled with being overweight for a lot of his life. And, before he put on weight, he reminded me some of the character Ralphie from the movie A Christmas Story. He being overweight and soft-looking made people underestimate him, and he used this to his advantage in a fight. In The Art of War, Sun Tzu said that all war is based on deception, so others were naturally deceived by Joe because of his appearance. And, there were other things that made people underestimate him. He was into what many kids in town would describe as nerdy endeavors such as collecting bugs and rocks.

However, I had seen him fight quite a few times and knew better. I remember watching him beat up a kid in a swimming pool, another on a football field. I asked him why he beat the kid up on the football field, and he said the guy said something bad about mom. Joe was very loyal to his family and protective of us as all my older brothers were. And though many considered Joe a nerd, Joe did sports, wresting being his favorite. One match when he was a sophomore in high school there were many who were doubting him because he was wresting against a guy who looked like a monster. And the guy threw Joe around most of the match, playing him like a yo-yo. However, Joe suddenly pinned the guy with a move called a Stack. The place went wild.

One day when I was a little kid I was playing with some of my neighborhood buddies. We liked to explore and roam around the neighborhoods. And, I was walking by the back fence of a house, and then suddenly on the inside of the fence a tall, very big, older redheaded kid named Brian raised up over the fence and threw a big rock down on top of my head. It took me by surprise, and I began crying and ran home and told my family about it. Joe was there and heard what happened. Brian was a grade ahead of Joe, but they knew each other because they played little league basketball on the same team. Immediately, Joe ran out of the house and went to the front door of Brian's house and rang the doorbell. I followed not too far behind in order to see what was going to happen.

Brian's dad answered the door and said, "Hello, Joe, how can I help you?"

"Hello, Mr. Gimper, is Brian here?" asked Joe.

"Yes, let me get him for you, just a moment," said Mr. Gimper who then went inside the house to get Brian.

Brian came to the door, and as soon as Joe saw him Joe grabbed him and dragged him to the front lawn and sat on him and began punching Brian very quickly back and forth with his left and right fists. Brian began screaming, "Help dad! Please get him off me. Help!" Brian was a much bigger kid than Joe, but that didn't matter. Like others, Brian also underestimated Joe. Brian's dad ran to the front door and saw the scene and immediately began trying to pull Joe off of Brian, but Joe seemed like a machine on a mission; and he continued to pound Brian's face.

Eventually, Mr. Gimper pulled Joe off of Brian and said, "What on earth are you doing? Why did you attack my son?"

"He threw a big rock down on my little brother's head," said Joe.

"Brian, is that true?" asked Mr. Gimper.

"Yes, but his little brother was trying to climb the fence and get in our backyard," said Brian.

"That's not true. He and his friends were just walking by the outside of your fence," said Joe.

"Well, I'm gonna go talk to your father about this Joe," said Mr. Gimper. Then, Brian's dad took Brian into their house and shut the door.

I watched this whole scene from a short distance and was very proud of my brother Joe. Mr. Gimper went and talked to my dad, and my dad was polite but told him that his son Brian deserved it. Mr. Gimper wasn't happy about that either. I don't know why he thought that he could convince my dad that his son Brian was a saint.

It was nice having my oldest brother Joe look out for me. Later in life, Joe passed away from a heart attack. The other night I watched a documentary on John Candy who was one of my favorite actors because he reminded me some of my brother Joe. When I meet an overweight person, I often think of my brother Joe. I have never been overweight, but I have compassion for people who struggle with weight issues because I saw how my bother Joe struggled with it. And, Joe had lost a lot of weight not too long before he passed away, and I was proud of him for losing a lot of weight. Joe was such a good person who had a lot of friends and would help anyone if they needed it, especially his family. My brother Joe was a great man, and I loved him and miss him dearly.

"Family on the Line"

The conflict with Coach Libe really began when one of my older brothers didn't go play football for the college where Coach Libe wanted him to go to. Instead, my brother chose a different college to go play football for. And, because of that Coach Libe held a grudge against my parents whom he blamed for that. So, he mostly tried to take it out on me in order to take a swing at them. He had retired from being the head football coach but for only a year. During that year he didn't coach, I was seventeen and a junior in high school and the starting varsity quarterback, and Coach Libe would go to the games and loudly bad mouth me in the stands. I heard this from a reliable source. So, when Coach Libe decided to become the head coach again, I didn't want to play for him and got a petition to try and stop him from becoming head coach again. Many signed the petition, and it also caused some controversy.

Coach Libe was feared by his players and many of the townspeople. He had a long winning record which made him popular to a certain degree, but there were also many who didn't like how he coached. Coach Libe not only looked formidable being very tall and muscular with blond hair, he was known for cheating, playing psychological games, his temper, and cruelty. He would make his players fight for positions and also would beat up certain players during practice. I felt sorry for players whose parents let Coach Libe beat them up and also players who didn't have parents to protect them. Coach Libe would bounce around the field during practice, and nobody would know whom he was going to hit. And, then suddenly he would hit a player. He did this to my oldest brother and tore his face mask off.

And, he liked to use fear to motivate his players, and they'd be so afraid of losing because if they did then they knew they would be punished in practice. The practices lasted a long time with a lot of conditioning, and at the end of the practice there was usually a performance from Coach Libe. He would lecture, cry, scream, threaten, and preach. He would have been a great actor. As players, we would sit there on one knee and listen to this into the night, and no one was allowed to move. So, the mosquitoes had field days feasting on our arms and legs.

It wasn't his looniness and brutality that made me not want to play for him even though there were those who said I didn't want to play for him because he was tough and made players work hard. No, I wasn't afraid of that. I had tougher coaches who demanded hard work before and got along with them fine. It was the conflict that I saw Coach Libe had with my parents and also the bad mouthing he did about me that made me not want to play for him. He was just trying to hurt my parents by bad mouthing me in public, but I didn't like being insulted and was also very protective of my parents.

So, when I got the petition against him, he became livid, and he called me into his office since he was the Athletic Director. There was an assistant coach there too. Though Coach Libe was a lot bigger than me, I was not intimidated by him and had no fear, even when he locked the door. He said to me, "Why did you get a petition against me?" I could see when he mentioned the word petition his face reacted with anger which he then tried to repress.

"I don't want to play for you," I said.

"What do you mean? Your brothers played for me and you did your sophomore year. There was never a problem. So, why now?" he asked.

"Mr. Jones said you went to the games and bad mouthed me in the stands," I said.

"I don't know why Mr. Jones told you that. What did he say that I said?" he asked.

"He said that you said that I sucked," I said.

"I never said you sucked," he said.

"Why would he make something like that up?" I asked.

"Look, I have never had an impure thought in my entire life," he said.

"I don't think you'll be fair with me. I'm the starting quarterback, and I've been the starting quarterback and leader of this team since the seventh grade; and I don't want you taking that and my team away from me. This is my team," I said.

"Well, I'm not sure if you will be my starting quarterback. You might trade time with the backup quarterback. You and your parents and the back-up quarterback and his parents may need to sit down with me, all of us together and discuss it," he said.

"No, I can't take the risk of you trying to ruin my senior year. I'm the quarterback. I will go away my senior year and play somewhere else," I said. Then, I looked him in the eyes and said with an emphasis, "I will not let you ruin my senior year."

That meeting happened in the spring, and the next couple months the conflict grew partly because nobody before had ever stood up to Coach Libe. Also, my dad drove me to meet two other coaches in the conference who had played against me and knew how good I was, so they wanted me to be their starting quarterback. And, word got out about that, so at a track meet Coach Libe got into a shouting match with one of those coaches and said that if I went to play for his team then he would make sure his players broke both of my legs when they played against me. That coach called up my dad and told him that. And, my parents also got a call that was a death threat even though they never told me about that call until many years later.

So, my parents could see that sending me to a nearby town to play in the same conference would have caused more problems. I was ambivalent about it. On one hand, I had fantasies about playing against my old teammates and Coach Libe while I listened to Aldo Nova's song "Fantasy," and on the other hand I didn't want to play against my old teammates whom I grew up with and loved. They had always looked to me as their quarterback and leader, and I didn't want to disappoint them. I wasn't just the starting quarterback. I had also been the starting point guard in basketball, and the point guard is like the quarterback on the basketball court. However, my parents and I eventually decided it would be best if I went away my senior year and play out of state. And, that's what I did and enjoyed my senior year of football. I had a head coach who loved me, and I loved him; and I was given an award for being the most valuable offensive player in football and also made Second Team All-State Quarterback in football my senior year. My parents put an article in the local newspaper which was about me being Second Team All-State Quarterback in football.

My parents cried the morning I left for my senior year, but they knew they were doing the right thing. Coach Libe and his staff didn't believe that I would really go away to play somewhere else. They had a meeting to discuss how they would handle it when I came back. However, I didn't return home to play football like they thought I would my senior year. I played elsewhere out of state and ended up staying there for my whole senior year because I loved it so much. I didn't have any time to think about Coach Libe anymore. Right after football, I played basketball making First Team All-Conference in basketball and then did Track. And, my parents also put an article in the local paper which was about me making First Team All-Conference in basketball.

After Coach Libe's football team had a bad season and word got out about my success elsewhere, Coach Libe told people that he didn't understand why I went away and that I would have been his starting quarterback without any doubt and that he was just trying to motivate me. And, I knew that I wouldn't have been able to do what I did if my family had not been blocking for me.

"The Cat with the Cue Tip"

My name is Toothy. They call me Toothy because I show my fangs a lot which are sharp and ferocious. I sit on the window ledge of the front window in the living room and show my fangs as people walk by, and they are scared because they pwentend to ignore me and keep walking by. I'm a beautiful gwey and white kitty. I don't want to say too much about it because I don't want to come acwoss as a bwaggart, but I think people should pay me to wook at me. My mommie found me on the stweet of Bisbee, Arizona. I don't wemember much about where I came from. I know I had a weal sissy whom I became separated fwom. You notice how I say whom instead of who. I am very articuwate. Anyways, this eighteen-year-old gwill actually found me and gave me to mommie.

I wuv pwaying with cue tips. I will knock over twash cans just to get a cue tip. My favorite singers are Pwince and Faith Hill. My favorite gwoop is Iron Maiden. The story I'm about to tell you is twew. I don't know why I'm telling you. I guess I just needed to exspwess myself. I once saw something very stwange at the house next door one night threw a side window of our house in my mommie's bedroom. When mommie fell asweep holding me, I got up and went to wook out the bedroom window. See, I only stay inside and wish I could go outside to catch some nice, delicious mice. Also, it would be nice to way in the Arizona sunshine and feel the wind bwow. That would be exciting and spiritual. And, to prowl at night would be ecstasy.

Anyways, I was sitting on the window ledge that night when I heard and saw two men outside. One man was rotund, and the other was gaunt. Now, you pwobably wonder why a kitty knows words like that. Well, I'm no ordinary kitty. I was born with a very high IQ, and my mommie is an English pwofessor; so I wisten to her conversations with her collweegs and enjoy the bwain candy. I awso wike the gweat witewary witers and philosophers. Wite now I am enjoying existentialism. So, it began when I saw these two humans outside at night. Next door is a kind of a cwappy house, and I don't know why the two guys would want to burglarize it; but they did. But, the biggest mistake is when the gaunt one kicked Wox on their way out. See, Wox is my boyfriend and lives there, but they wet him wun around outside. He's an indoor and outdoor cat wike Tarzan. He's a big handsome brown Tabby cat and could be an actor if he wanted to.

Stealing is unethwical too. One of my sissies once twied to steal a cue tip from me, and I had to fight her off. Well, I might as well tell you about my two sissies. They aren't my weal sissies. Mommie got them later after she had me for about siss months. I enjoyed the pwace to myself for a wong time, and now theres these two little sissies that I have to share stuff with. They are both white cats. However, one is a girly girl, and the other is a tom boy. The girly gwill is a southern belle and wikes Kenny Chesney. She keeps saying she loves Kenny Chesney and wants to go to Nashville. And, I keep saying to her go ahead. My other sissy likes Debbie Boone. The girly girl is a wibetarian and a Southern Baptist, and the tom boy is a Democwat and Methowist. I'm a staunch wepublican and a Cathowick. Anyways, I'm the smallest one, physically, but I'm a gwate athwete, like a gymnast, and can wun fast and jump willy high. Also, l'm tough wike Billy Jack. I wuv how bikers twy to mess with Billy, and Billy stays calm and says stuff like, "Why aren't you boys in church?" and then beats them up. I'm not afwaid of anything. Sometimes loud noises make me go hide, but that's about it. However, if I needed to, I'd beat up the loud noises too.

So, each night I would watch out the window kinda wike Jimmy Stewart in *Rear Window*, and I noticed that this house was being burglarized that night when the people who lived there were gone. Wox tried to stop them as they went out the door, and the gaunt one kicked Wox. Wox wan over to my window for help, but what could I do? I was twapped in the house. I twied to wake my mommie, but she was in a deep sweep.

That weekend though, my mommie went out of town to a witerwary conference to pwesent her paper on Virginia Woolf, and the same two humans bwoke into our house. My sissies wan and hid under the couch because they were scaredy cats, but not me. I got up on the wefwigewator and scrunched down in the dark and patiently waited wike a gwate hunter. Then, at the wite time, I jumped on the back of the neck of the gaunt one who kicked Wox. I sunk my fangs deep into his neck wike a vampire, and he screamed and caused a big commotion, stumbling around and knocking over things, trying to throw me off the back of his neck. However, I wouldn't wet go. The rotund guy yelled at him to shut up.

But, you won't beweive what happened next, but it's twew. My sissies came out of hiding from under the couch and attached the back wegs of the rotund guy and also wouldn't wet go, so then he started screaming too. I must admit that I was pwowd of my sissies for overcoming being a scaredy cat. A neighbor called the police, and the police arrived and arrested the two buggards. I meowed to the gaunt one as the police shuffled them off in handcuffs, "That was for Wox!" And, there was an article about it in a wocal newspaper which said my sissies and I are hewoes with our pictures next to the article though it was just an excuse for me to be wooked at. Like I said, I'm a beautiful kitty. And, wite before the newspaper photogwapher snapped the camwa, I flashed him my indomitable fangs.

"Small Town Web"

Four girls ran the small town of Larkney, Texas, and it seemed like every guy was in love with them. They were the Nelson sisters, and their dad was a rich oil man who spoiled them. Their dad had also been a head football coach there and had won five state championships in football before he went into the family oil business. His youngest daughter Charlotte was my girlfriend for a while in high school. I was a year ahead of her. She didn't like the guys in her own grade and never dated them. The so-called studs in her grade resented her and I think secretly wished she would at least give them some attention too.

Charlotte was cute, but there were other girls in town that would be considered more attractive than her by society's standards. It is an odd thing how a less attractive girl can be the queen bee and have the guys jumping at her every command when there are other girls more attractive than her who stand aside and watch. And, she didn't have the kind of sex appeal that a lot of guys like. She was tall with black hair and grey eyes, but she wasn't athletic and well built like some of the other girls. One other girl was considered the most beautiful in the town and had a crush on me and let me know it often, but I wasn't interested in her. Attraction seems mysterious, but there is some logic behind it.

Charlotte was charismatic and the leader of the girls in her grade who followed her. She would sometimes try to set her friends up with my friends. Charlotte had supreme confidence, more so than the other girls by a lot, moving about with swan-like grace, and she was chic because she was posh and could afford it. Her dad gave her five hundred dollars every two weeks just for an allowance. I didn't even have an allowance. But, for some reason she was also a kleptomaniac and had been caught several times. This was common knowledge in town, but she didn't seem to care. It was probably her way of saying I can do what I want. Although, one time when she was caught she first called me instead of her parents. I don't know what she thought

I could do about it. I was just a high school student and from a poor family. I think she might have been showing off.

Charlotte had other things that made her appealing to guys. Besides being cute, well-dressed and from a rich, powerful family in town, she had a dynamic personality. She wasn't shy in anyway, but she didn't speak a whole lot; however, when she did speak people would listen. And, she knew how to get attention by being a drama queen at times. If she was upset about something, then she didn't hold back. I didn't hold that against her. I think it is good for people to be able to express themselves like that when needed. However, she would take it pretty far.

One time, I heard she had kissed another guy, so I was ignoring her. Thus, to get my attention she went into the boy's locker room where I was getting changed for football practice, along with the rest of the team, just to explain to me that the guy she had kissed was just a friend and it was only a small friendship peck on the cheek. She said some others had seen it and were gossiping about it and lying about the type of the kiss it was as an attempt to break us up. When the coach saw her there in the boy's locker room, he got mad at me and treated her like she was royalty. She could get away with things like that, and nobody would question it. Everyone knew whom her drug dealer was, but nobody asked her about it, not even me.

And, though charming, she could be complicated and cruel. She went through a lot of boyfriends. When she would find a new boyfriend, she would write her current boyfriend a letter and let them know she was breaking up with them for another guy. She wouldn't tell them to their face. I thought that was cruel, but she should of at least told, them to their face. I once saw a popular big strong jock bawling over her which was surreal, and I wondered if she enjoyed breaking the hearts of guys.

I first talked to her on a choir trip on the back of the school bus. We got to talking, and I could tell she liked me even though she had a boyfriend at the time in my same grade who was considered a stud.

And, sure enough, she wrote the guy a letter and told him that she was breaking up with him in order for I to be her new boyfriend. I know this because the guy read the letter to his friends, and I was standing not too far away and heard the whole thing. He said he didn't care, but I knew he did. At the time, it didn't bother me. However, looking back now, it has always bothered me. I shouldn't have gone along with it. At the time, I suppose I was blinded by infatuation. She asked me if I wanted to go steady, and I said yes.

Thus, we spent a lot of time together as an official couple, mostly would make-out and hold hands, or I'd put my arm around her and walk around campus with her. And, we went to the movies a lot, such as to see the movie *Pretty in Pink*, and in that movie the song "If you Leave" by OMD was considered our song. While we were watching that movie, she kept her hand on my knee the whole time. One time she moved her hand from my knee during that movie, and my knee felt like ice until she put her hand on it again. After a while we broke up, but then I beat up a big guy that many were talking about in town; and so she wanted to get back together with me, and I said yes.

Most of the time we were together she didn't say much, but there was one night at a house party after a play that we were both in that she opened up to me more. For most of the night she hung out with her friends, and I sat across the room and waited for her to join me. Eventually, she got up and told her friends she had to go see me and walked over to me. For some privacy we went outside to talk in the backyard. Then I said to her, "Why are you with me?"

"What do you mean?" she asked.

"I come from a poor family and don't belong to your church. My family is considered outsiders in this town," I said.

"So?" she responded.

"And, I don't understand why you have had a ton of boyfriends. It seems like they are like toys for you to play with until you get tired of them," I said.

She kept quiet for a while and then spoke, "What's the problem?"

"I'm serious," I said.

"Look, I really like you, but you are a complex guy. Why do you get upset at me for my past and for being who I am. The reason you like me is because of who I am. If I wasn't Charlotte Nelson, then you'd probably not like me. And, do you think it is easy being me?" she asked and was starting to get upset.

"What do you mean?" I asked.

"I'm a Nelson girl, and we have to act in a certain way because that's what people in this town expect. My sisters say the same thing. I want to leave this town and go somewhere else where nobody knows who I am," she said.

"Pretty is as pretty does," I said.

"What's that supposed to mean?" she asked.

"Because of your status in town, you have the power to do good things for people. But, you don't. Instead, you are shallow and cruel. Everyone knows it, but they just accept it which encourages it even more. You probably like me just because I'm considered good-looking and also the quarterback," I said.

"Wow! Where did all that come from? Why are you even with me if you think that? Is that really what you think of me?" she asked.

"Isn't that true?" I asked and could see her getting more upset with tears.

"You know I wouldn't be with you if you weren't good-looking. Why did you want me to say it? Do you like torturing me? So, I'm shallow. And, I'm cruel! Deal with it!" she screamed. I began looking around to see if anyone was listening. And, I became angry and then sad and didn't say anything. She could see my reaction and then spoke up again, "You know what your problem is?"

"No," I said.

"You act self-righteous. However, you are just as shallow, and you can be cruel, but won't admit these things," she said.

"I haven't had a lot of girlfriends," I said.

"All the girls have liked you, but you were too picky," she said.

"I had no control over them liking me. I didn't use them," I said.

"That's because you are a serious guy with a big ego who only likes bimbos," she said.

"You're not a bimbo," I said.

"No, I'm not a bimbo, but that's the image I have; and you know that. I know how people see me and my older sisters. I'm not the kind of girl your mother would approve of," she said.

"I see a lot in you that others can't see," I said and began to feel sorry for her.

She then began to dry her tears and laughed, "That's what others have said, but I think you probably mean it knowing how serious you are."

"The problem is religion," I said.

She then remained silent and after a while said, "I'm going back inside to the party."

"I think I'll stay out here awhile," I said.

She went back inside, and I stayed outside in the backyard in the dark by myself for a while looking up at the stars and wondering how insignificant our relationship probably was compared to outer space, but my relationship with Charlotte was like a vast inner space with a web of powerful chaotic emotions that could be overwhelming like how I was feeling that night. Loud music was coming from the house party which was the song "The Sun Always Shines on TV" by A-ha, which was another one of our songs, and I felt the song running through my mind. However, after the song, instead of going back into the house party, I left and went home.

And, the relationship didn't last. When I think about her now, I wonder how she is doing but mostly think about how bad I still feel for the guy she broke up with to be with me.

"The Sentimentalist"

Ted and Sid entered and sat down to eat dinner together in The Olive Garden in Nashville, Tennessee. Ted was a short, stocky guy with long blond hair, and Sid was a tall, overweight guy with short black hair. They were both in their twenties and graduate students. They agreed to meet up for dinner to discuss Friedrich Nietzsche's concept of the eternal recurrence. After the waiter took their orders, Sid said to Ted, "You see the difference between me and you from the others up there in the department is that we're dialectical thinkers."

Ted responded, "Ya your right. How can one be post-modern at a Christian university?"

Sid knew that Ted meant it as a rhetorical question but began to answer the question; however, Ted interrupted him, "Sid, I'm messed up."

"How's that?" asked Sid.

"Everyone, everything outside of myself is telling me to go back to my wife, so I'm the only one in this world who thinks I should leave her," said Ted.

"Ya," said Sid.

Also I don't want to ruin her life. It's all me. I wish I could show her how she would be better off without me, so I wouldn't feel all this guilt," said Ted.

"Ya, man, I can't tell you what to do," said Sid.

I'm gonna be like you. We're both becomers; nobody understands us here. The others are be-ers," said Ted.

"Ya, you remind me of Rabbit in John Updike's novel *Rabbit, Run*. Rabbit leaves his wife, and everyone is trying to get him to go back to her. Rabbit tells the minister that God wants a waterfall to not be a tree. A waterfall is becoming while a tree is fixed. See what I mean?" asked Sid. Sid liked applying everything to literature or philosophy which Ted understood and expected because Ted was similar in that way.

"Ya! I need to read that." said Ted.

"Ah, what was the main thing that made you separate from her?" asked Sid.

Ted answered, "I just don't think I can truly experience the joy that I'm capable of experiencing. Also, there's a problem of intimacy. I just wish she would show more affection."

"Ya, I understand. I think that's why you try to get people to open up and show emotion, maybe because you cannot get it from your wife. It's strange how your dogs are like you and your wife. One is outgoing, and the other is aloof," said Sid.

"You and I are both sentimentalists, and these hard-boiled people don't understand us," said Ted.

"So what are you gonna do?" asked Sid.

"I'll probably go home," said Ted.

"I think you should go somewhere where nobody knows you. Go west? How about San Francisco? You see you need to go somewhere there will be people you can talk to about the same stuff you're interested in. You're welcome to go wherever I go," said Sid.

"We should go live in Germany and study Nietzsche. So anyways, you said you wanted to know how chaos fits into Nietzsche's eternal becoming. I guess it just means that all is meaningless and only those who can accept this can overcome it. That existence is all fire, flux and conflict, and existence is so heavy that it will be repeated over and over for eternity. Are you ready to accept that? That this conversation we are having now will occur forever," said Ted.

"Even the most interesting conversation would get boring fast. I don't know if I can accept that," said Sid sarcastically. The waiter then brought the food, and Sid started to pray.

"Tell Jesus hi for me," said Ted.

"I pray for my food because I didn't create it," said Sid.

"I see," said Ted.

"You know the way I've changed the way I look at God really has helped me," said Sid.

"How so?" asked Ted.

"In Alice Walker's novel *The Color Purple*, Shug Avery says that God is in everything," said Sid.

"That's pantheism," stated Ted.

"No not the way I see it. I mystify everything. That helps me. Basically, all life is created by God, and therefore it needs to be nurtured and taken care of; and anything that destroys it is evil," said Sid.

"Nature is a paradox. It nurtures and destroys. Nature is cruel. Haven't you ever seen a cat play with a grasshopper before it killed it? I don't know Sid. Life is a tragedy," said Ted.

"There does seem to be no pattern to this universe. Nothing makes sense. However, just because it looks like it doesn't make sense doesn't mean there's no meaning to it. I think a chaotic universe reinforces the boundless capacity of God's power," said Sid.

"But, how can you believe in God when nothing makes sense?" asked Ted.

"Kierkegaard explains that the leap of faith is irrational. It's not supposed to make sense," said Sid.

"I wish I knew why us sentimentalists have to suffer," said Ted.

"It seems like with all great writers what sets them apart was they were sentimental for whatever reason. The reasons vary of course. It's tough being vulnerable. I can't fit into the American model of manhood. You know, the kind Saul Bellow describes in his first novel *Dangling Man*. As you know, only what Bellow calls the hard-boiled can fit into hard-boiledom. The other night I was watching a movie at Tylor's house, and there was this one scene in this movie that disturbed me so much I got up and walked home ten miles at 3 in the morning. Nobody even came and got me. I guess they thought I was being a wimp," said Sid.

Ted replied, "I know what you mean. The other night at Calvin's house we were drinking, and Calvin grabs Sergie by the throat; and I went into the other room and broke down and cried. I couldn't believe humans can be so cruel."

An older man of average height and build with short red hair had been sitting alone in a booth next to where Sid and Ted were sitting and had been carefully listening the whole time to their conversation. And, when he got up to leave, he said to them, "Hey boys, sentimentalism sounds great. Where can I get some?"

"See what I mean?" Ted says to Sid.

"I'll make you cry," said Sid to the older man.

"Do it?" requested the older man.

Sid stood up and hugged the older man, and the older man began to weep.

"Hide your Computer"

It was the Wednesday before Thanksgiving break, and Troy strutted up to the front of the World Literature class that he was taking to give his presentation on some aspect of Milan Kundera's novel The Unbearable Lightness of Being. He had his paper in one hand and a box in the other hand. He was dressed up in a black and white suit and had a look of conviction. He had short platinum blond hair and was tall, big, strong and athletic. He stood six foot six and weighed over 300 pounds. He played football and also threw the shot put and disc for the college. He considered himself a "thinking brute." He had told people that he despised the so called "idiots" on the football team but also the "weak nerds" in his English classes. He liked to pride himself on being what he described as a paradox and the only player on the football team who wrote poetry. He called himself a "philosophical red-neck."

A lot of women were drawn to him even though he would get in arguments in class about feminism. He would say that feminism is destroying masculinity and things like that about it which made the professor Dr. Billings and some students in the class upset, most of them women. However, a lot of women still liked him, and he dated several women. He said it was because deep down women wanted a real man like himself. Because of him, some students enjoyed going to class, and some dreaded it. He had a polarizing personality.

Troy was a Milan Kundera fan and had started a Kundera club where they would read Kundera's novels and discuss them. He couldn't get any of his teammates to join the club except for his roommate Kevin, but he did find some others from his classes to join. The club took it very seriously and had spent weeks discussing Kundera's novel *The Book of Laughter and Forgetting*, and now they were on Kundera's novel *The Unbearable Lightness of Being*. They had just watched the film based on it and discussed that too at a member's house. This member of the club was one of the women that

Troy was dating. And, in class Troy talked a lot about Kundera, so it was no surprise to many that day when he got up to present about an aspect in Kundera's novel *The Unbearable Lightness of Being*. He held up the box and said, "In this box I hold the totality of all human knowledge." The class was a little nervous about seeing what was in the box.

He then took out a dry cow patty and said, "This cow patty is the totality of all human knowledge.", and some of the class began laughing. Troy became angry by the laughter and said, "Shut up! I'm serious about this shit. Listen to me. Life is cyclical: we die and fertilize the soil to help the grass grow, and then the cows eat the grass and defecates us back out. All things work toward crap. In the novel *The Unbearable Lightness of Being,* Milan Kundera talks about the kingdom of kitsch. The kingdom of kitsch is the denial of shit. Basically, it means the denial of what society or our super-ego calls the low in life. If we can accept crap, then we accept ourselves. Friedrich Nietzsche's idea of the eternal recurrence is a test for the overman. If the overman can accept his excrement, then he has passed Nietzsche's psychological test, ultimately finding joy and acceptance with his position in the universe. Now, are there any questions?"

The class was quiet, even the ones that Troy would often argue with. Dr. Billings liked for his class to have a discussion after each presentation, so he also asked if the class had any questions, but the class still remained silent because they were in shock. Dr. Billings was too. Dr. Billings was a short man in his sixties with long grey hair in a ponytail and wore glasses. He had been a professor for a long time and thought he had seen everything, until Troy came along; although, his experience had taught him to also stay calm and keep the class engaged. So, when the class still remained mute after he asked for any questions a second time, Dr. Billings forced enough bravado to address Troy, "I have a question."

"Yes, Dr. Billings. What is your question?" asked Troy.

Dr. Billings responded, "Although scat is part of existence, I don't think it is the totality of all human knowledge. According to what you just said it is important for one to accept one's feces. However, isn't it just important for one to accept other aspects of existence as well? If so, then cow excrement is only part of the grand scale. Am I not right?"

Troy answered, "No, not at all. If one can accept one's crap, then that leads to all acceptance, because let's face it. Accepting one's feces is the most difficult task of all. And I'm not just talking about literal but the crap we run from. According to Nietzsche, in order for one to accept oneself then one must confront every humiliating, terrible, and tragic aspect of one's past. If one was to deny any of one's past, then one is wishing to become another person. The low is what we must accept because let's face it: we all return to the earth. Gravity pushes us down and not up. See, the unbearable lightness of being which Kundera talks about is the emptiness one feels when isolated from the earth and one's body. This lightness of being which we desire does not exist. It is only a way to escape the weight of existence. We cannot escape existence. We must embrace our crap. The first step is to eat our post-food." Then, Troy took a bite out of the cow patty. Some of the class were grossed out. One student even started gagging and ran out of the classroom. And, some started clapping. The professor Dr. Billings wasn't clapping and told Troy that he wanted to speak to him after class.

So, Troy stayed after class to talk to Dr. Billings. Dr. Billing said to him, "That was some presentation you gave, interesting but inappropriate like your Jacques Derrida presentation you gave in my Literary Criticism class last spring."

"You just didn't understand Derrida," said Troy.

"No, it wasn't that. I didn't like how you let off a firecracker in class in order to illustrate an aporia in a text. I warned you then, but you didn't learn your lesson," said Dr. Billings.

"The class liked it. Nobody complained about it to me but you," said Troy.

"Well, this time, you may have noticed a student ran out of class. You really like to shock people. Don't you?" asked Dr. Billings.

Troy responded, "I was just trying to get my point across. I succeeded if I get a bad grade on it. I think it was Martin Buber who said that if people tell you that you're wrong then that means you're doing something right."

"It was interesting, but, again, you should have first told me what you were going to do. Please don't do that again," said Dr. Billings.

"Ya, like you would have approved it. I knew you'd hate it," said Troy.

"I didn't hate it. I thought it was interesting, but you didn't need to eat cow dung to get your point across. Like I told you before, you need to learn to be more civil. Please try to be more sympatico. Think of the other students and not just yourself. Don't be selfish. You should have learned that before now, but since you didn't then that should be a primary goal in your education. You can't coerce your ideas on people by trying to shock them," said Dr. Billings.

"You're just like all the other Marxist professors," said Troy.

"Excuse me? That is not apropos to the issue we are discussing. What does Marx have to do with any of this?" asked Dr. Billings.

"You professors here are all the same, extremely liberal and bias. Like with feminism. You get your feathers ruffled whenever I say anything negative about it," said Troy.

"No, I don't. I stay impartial, like always. I don't tell students what my political views are. I haven't heard any other student say what you're saying," said Dr. Billings.

"That's because the other students are too afraid to speak up about it. I have seen how some students have tried to hide their conservative views in your class," said Troy.

"Like I said, I never heard that. Please stop trying to create a canard. If I ever seem to get upset toward you, then it's just because I don't like your overly rude and aggressive attitude which is disrespectful toward other students and me. Please don't ever tell the class to shut up again or try to shock them," said Dr. Billings.

"I'm just being myself. Why can't men be men? Look what feminism has done to you. Feminism is crap," said Troy.

"If you really believe that then you should embrace it because you said we must embrace scat," said Dr. Billings.

That night Troy told his roommate Kevin about what happened in his class and his conversation with Dr. Billings. Kevin was a big, strong guy with short red hair, and though he was taller than Troy he wasn't as strong and athletic as Troy. Kevin strongly reacted to what Troy told him, "No way! That's some crazy caca! Why did you eat a cow turd in front of the class? You didn't tell me you were gonna do that. You'll probably get kicked out of the university for that."

"I don't care. I had to make a point. Words are pointless without action. People like Dr. Billings just like to sit around and talk about ideas but never do anything. It's just a word game to him. I don't want to be like that. I had to do something that they will remember. If you shock people, they will be more likely to remember it. I didn't plan on it. Early before the class I got to thinking that I needed to do something more to make my presentation stronger, and the idea came to me. I remembered the cow pasture not too far from here and drove over there and quickly got it and put it in a box. Even then, I just planned on showing it to the class during my presentation. Then, I just let my instinct take over which is a good thing," said Troy.

"Well, I'm sure people will remember it. But, I can't believe you're willing to risk losing your football scholarship and getting kicked out of school for some dumb idea," said Kevin.

"It's not a dumb idea. I want to wake people up and get them to confront reality and who they really are. I wouldn't expect you to understand. You're just a business major and don't even read great writers. And besides, Jack Kerouac lost his football scholarship and dropped out of college," said Troy.

"Just because I told you I never read Spinoza, you assume I'm some dumb brute who hasn't read anything. Of course, I've read a lot of great writers. I told you I'm a business major in order to please my parents. I want to make a difference too, but I don't eat crap. Look, you'll probably get kicked out of here, so you might as well do something that would really make a difference," said Kevin. Troy heard what Kevin said, but Troy wasn't really listening because he had begun worrying about what his coaches would think when they find out.

"My coaches are gonna be pissed when they hear about it," said Troy then imaged Dr. Billings telling the Dean what occurred in class that day. He figured since it was the second time Dr. Billings was upset at him for being too shocking in class then it was just a matter of time that Dr. Billings would report it to the Dean and then the Dean would tell his head football coach. After all, Dr. Billings had warned him before. It was November, and the football team had gone undefeated so far. Troy knew that the team counted on him because he was a starting defensive tackle, but still his ideas were more important to him than sports.

"Hey, I got an idea. I know the Resident Assistant, and I could borrow his key to every dorm room over Thanksgiving break. I'll give him back the key after the break. But, during the break, we could steal stuff and then destroy it," said Kevin.

"Why would he let you borrow the key?" asked Troy.

"I have some serious dirt on him," said Kevin.

"What did he do?" asked Troy.

"I told him I would never tell, but if he doesn't let me borrow the key then I'll tell him that I changed my mind," said Kevin.

"Wow, that's a brilliant idea! But, you're just joking, right?" asked Troy.

"No, I'm not. I've actually been thinking about it for a while now," said Kevin.

"Yes, we could make a statement against materialism, capitalism and technology. Become humanitarian soldiers fighting against the machine which has separated the bonds of brotherhood. Teach people a lesson. Show them that nothing belongs to them. Free them from their isolation from one another and themselves and unite them with what is real--their instincts, love and emotion," said Troy.

"Exactly! Like Computers! Computers are also artificial, and we'd be helping people become a little less phony. We'll steal computers and take them into the woods and shoot them," said Kevin.

"Yes, but we'll use baseball bats. That will be more primitive. We must get back to our instincts. Instead of a catcher in the rye like Holden Caulfield, we'll be a basher in the woods," said Troy.

"The gun was invented way before baseball," said Kevin.

"Don't be a smart-mouth. You know what I mean," said Troy.

So, Kevin was able to borrow the key, and over Thanksgiving break Troy and Kevin stole computers from dorm rooms and took them out in the woods and destroyed them by smashing them with baseball bats. They liked feeling barbaric and thinking they were doing it for a good purpose.

The Monday after Thanksgiving break, Troy was back in Dr. Billing's class. After class, Troy asked Dr. Billings if he was in

trouble, and Dr. Billings told him no. Troy then went back to his dorm
room, and the police were there with Kevin waiting for Troy.

"Facing the Sun"

Late at night in July, Fred was drunk and went into the mountains to die. He had walked many miles from his house with no shoes and socks on, and his bare feet were bloodied; however, he didn't care. He stumbled around the mountains in the dark and then lied down on his back and tried to go to sleep. But, he couldn't sleep. His mind was racing, and he kept thinking about how his wife betrayed him.

Fred was a handsome short, thin man with short brown hair and was an important man in the town on the edge of the mountains. Even though he was a lawyer, most of the townspeople loved him. He wouldn't turn down cases even if he knew he wouldn't make much money from it like other lawyers did. He did that because he wanted to help poor people. Because of that, he wasn't wealthy like other lawyers, but he was respected and admired. He got along with most everyone, and people generally liked to be around him. He had always loved the town since he moved there with his family when he was in high school, and so he was easily persuaded by his wife to move back there after he graduated from law school.

As he lied there alone on his back in the mountains with no shoes on in a t-shirt with blue jeans on, he kept wondering why his wife betrayed him. They had married twelve years ago, and he was now thirty-two. His wife was the same age as him, and they were high school sweethearts. He was from back east and felt like an outsider in the western town when he first moved there, and his wife was from there. There were families there that had been there for many generations, and his wife was from one of those families. When he converted to her religion and married her, they treated him like he was one of them, but he still always felt like an outsider, like an imposter. His parents didn't want him to marry her or leave their religion that they had brought him up in. So, he always felt guilty for betraying his parents and was thinking that perhaps that was why his wife betrayed him. Though it was never said, he thought his wife could sense his guilt for marrying her. And, he wondered if his insecurity of always feeling like an outsider and his guilt for marrying her had eventually caused his wife to turn on him.

He was too drunk and tired to figure it out though, so he thought he would just lie there in the forest and starve to death or a bear or pack of wolves would find him. There were many wild animals in those mountains, and he had been hunting in them many times before with some of his wife's relatives. They liked to go deep into the mountains and drink and hunt together. He had been drunk many times in those mountains, but this time was different. In high school there were different locations where he and others would meet to party. The police in town were aware of those party spots, but they never would go there to break up the parties and just let the teenagers do their thing.

His wife had been faithful to him for five years, and after that she became known as the town tart. Fred pretended like he didn't know it, and he tried not to think about it. It was like he was living in a cave, somewhat like Plato's cave, and refused to walk outside and see the sun because it would blind him. The truth was too difficult for him to face because he was too in love with his wife. Thus, he never confronted his wife about it, and when people in town would tell him about it he would change the conversation or walk away.

One time, Fred was out of town working on a case, and his wife had a party at their house. During the party, she and two guys went into the bathroom, while another couple went and used the bed in the master bedroom where Fred and his wife slept. The couple turned the electric blanket on which was on the bed because the summer nights in the highly elevated town got cold, but the couple accidently left it on high which burned a hole in the mattress. When Fred discovered it on the mattress, his wife told him that she had left it on because she missed him so much that she wasn't thinking. Fred went shopping for a new mattress, and several of the workers in the store were sympathetic toward him. However, one worker there in the store who was at the party and knew about it kept snickering behind Fred's back and whispering snide remarks about Fred to other workers. But, the manager of the store liked Fred and heard about it, so the manager chastised the worker for it and threatened to fire him.

After three days of lying there on his back in the mountains, Fred still couldn't fall asleep. He had gone into the mountains because he finally had to face the truth. His wife had gotten pregnant by another man and wanted to leave him and be with this other man. The other man was another lawyer in his firm whom Fred had thought was his friend. Even though this other lawyer was arrogant and overly confident unlike Fred, Fred was a better lawyer. Fred used his hard work and analytical skills to win cases. He was wise about most things except when it came to his wife's infidelity. That was his only weakness. He had always been a romantic, and if he had married the right woman he would have been happy. There was another woman in town that always liked Fred, and this woman was kind and virtuous, but Fred didn't choose her because his wife had been more aggressive in the chase to win his heart. He recalled is wife telling the other woman that Fred wouldn't choose her because she was ugly. His wife was attractive, a tall blonde, but Fred thought the other woman was also beautiful. However, he also liked the fact that his wife came from a prominent family in town, and the other woman did not.

So, one morning Fred woke up, and his wife was standing by the bed with a suitcase and told him that she was pregnant and that she was leaving him for the other lawyer whom she said was the father. Fred became angry and began yelling at her, "I knew you were a strumpet! Everyone knows that! However, how do you even know whom the father is?"

"I know! You sure are not the father! You were sure never a husband to me either. And, ya, I am strumpet! So what? It's a free country. I can do whatever the hell I want, and nobody in town cares. Who cares if they did? Get over it! You're just a wimp! I have many men, and that's okay. We are one big family. They don't judge me like you. I want to be a courtesan," she said and left the room.

Fred stayed in bed that day in shock, and when night first arrived he began heavily drinking whiskey and later into the dark night began walking toward the mountains, staying off roads to not be seen. He had forgotten to put his shoes and socks on, but he didn't care.

While Fred was lying there on his back in the mountains waiting to die, he felt numb and also began thinking that he had been too nice of a guy. He had always gone along with what his wife had wanted. He was thinking that nice guys finish last, and even though they are loved by many it is the corrupt people in life who get what they want. He had never been that type of person. He was thinking that even if he tried to be cruel and selfish that he wouldn't be able to do it. He thought how unfair it was for him to be punished for being too conscientious. He was the type who wanted to please everyone. He pleased everyone but himself. Eventually though, he could no longer think coherently about that or anything else.

He had been lying now there in the wilderness for three days, and his face was brutally baked a deep red from the sun. The UV rays was high in the mountains during the hottest month, and the sun shined no mercy on him. His mind also began to betray him, and he imagined that the sun was his wife who was insulting him. For a while, he listened submissively like an obedient child, but then he began to change.

Deep inside him, he began to rage, and he wanted to fight. He began hollering at the sun whom he continued to think was his wife. He yelled, "You can't do this to me! I won't allow it anymore!" He had an overwhelming powerful feeling that he wanted to live and was going to fight. He tried to get up, but he couldn't. He couldn't even move. So, he started yelling, "Help Me!" which he kept repeating for hours.

Then, two young men hiking heard him calling out and followed his voice to find him. The two young men were camp counsellors from out of town and didn't know Fred. They were both good men and wanted to help Fred. One ran down the mountain to get help while the other one stayed with Fred. The one who stayed with Fred had never seen a man in that bad of shape. Fred was blinded by the sun. And, his lips were covered with sun blisters from being kissed by the sun whom Fred kept thinking was his wife. He repeated was yelling, "Stop kissing me!"

The young man didn't understand what Fred meant, but he stayed with Fred and was saying, "It's okay. You're gonna be okay. Help is on the way. Hang in there. I'm with you. I'm your friend and won't hurt you." The young man's voice was like cool water to Fred's tortured soul.

Eventually, the other young man who went to get help returned with some men from the fire department. The firemen and the young men who found Fred carried Fred a long way down the mountains to a dirt road where a firetruck was waiting for them. The young man who had stayed with Fred, while the other young man ran to get help, was helping the others carry Fred and kept praying in his mind to God that he wouldn't drop Fred, and he didn't. Nobody dropped Fred. They were able to save Fred, and Fred recuperated in the hospital. And, when Fred got out of the hospital, he saw the sun again and not his wife. He was happy and thankful to be alive, and he also had decided that after the divorce he was going to look up the kind virtuous woman that had liked him.

"The Cat in the Woods"

Ricky loved cats. He was too young yet to play sports with his older brothers, so he played a lot with the family cat; although, he could be obnoxious and liked to hide the cat in different uncomfortable places. His mother had to constantly keep an eye on little Ricky and referred to him as "Dennis the Menace." She also kept an open ear for the sound of meowing because she never knew where Ricky would hide the cat next. Thanks to hearing the cat meow, she had found the cat in the refrigerator and also another time in the dryer.

When Ricky would get in trouble for things like that, she would scold him, and he'd say he was sorry; however, it wouldn't be long before he got in trouble again. Ricky often disobeyed his parents, and sometimes he could get away with it because he was the youngest. One time, Ricky was in the back seat of the car with his older brothers, and he told his dad who was driving to shut up. Ricky's dad just started laughing. However, the mom in the front passenger's seat said to her husband, "You better do something about that now. If you don't, when he gets to be sixteen he will be very rebellious, and then it won't be funny."

Ricky was a five-years-old and had shaggy white hair. He was known for being a little cutie, and little girls in the neighborhood liked to chase him and kiss him when they caught him. And, besides the family cat, Ricky also liked to play with other cats in the neighborhood too.

There was a stray grey cat that lived in the woods behind the neighborhood, and Ricky also loved this cat and wanted to play with it. However, each time Ricky would get close to the cat, the cat would hiss and run away. Then, Ricky would get his feelings hurt because he didn't understand why the wild cat would run away from him.

One day he saw the cat underneath the car in their driveway, so he crawled underneath the car to pet the cat. He got close enough to the cat to pet it, but when he petted the cat on the cat's head, the cat hissed but didn't run away. Instead, the cat scratched up little Ricky and then stayed underneath the car. So, little Ricky began bawling and ran inside to his mom. His mom wiped away his tears and went outside to get a good look at the cat that scratched up her baby boy.

When Ricky's dad arrived home from work, he heard all about the incident from his wife. Together they decided to go report it to the Animal Control Service, and the man they spoke to about it there told them that the stray cat could have rabies. He told them that Ricky would have to start getting shots regularly in the stomach right way unless they could first prove that the stray cat didn't have rabies. And, he told them that the only way to determine that the cat had rabies or not was to have the cat killed and its head cut off and sent to a laboratory for testing. They told Ricky about it and asked him where they could find the cat. Ricky told them that he had seen the cat in the woods behind the neighborhood.

So, the father took his gun and went into the woods to find the cat. His wife went along in order to identify the cat, and they told Ricky to stay at the house. Once the mom identified the cat and pointed it out to her husband, she left and went back to the house. She didn't want to see her husband shoot the cat. The husband was a good shot and shot the cat with one shot. And, as he was carrying the dead cat out of the woods and back to his house, Ricky came running out to him. And, the father said to his son, "We told you to stay at the house. Why did you not obey us? You weren't supposed to see this."

"I came to stop you. I loved the kitty," said little Ricky as he began crying.

"I know, but I had to son. We explained this to you. I feel bad about it, but we have to see if the cat has rabies. If it doesn't have rabies, then you won't have to have regular shots in the stomach," said the father.

"But I'm tough. I can handle it, dad," said Ricky as he was still crying.

"I know you're tough, Ricky, but you shouldn't have to go through that if I can prevent it," said the father.

Then, there were a group of neighbors that also came walking up to the father as he was carrying the dead cat back to his house. One lady in the pack yelled, "Did you kill that cat?"

"Yes, I had to in order to find out if it has rabies. The cat scratched up my son," said the father.

"You should be ashamed of yourself killing an innocent helpless little animal like that! And, look at your son crying. What kind of example are you setting for your son?" asked the lady.

"I feel bad about it, but I'm trying to protect my son. He was just about to start having regular shots in the stomach for rabies. However, now that I've killed the cat and will have it tested, then there may be a chance that he won't have to start having regular shots in the stomach if the test results show the cat doesn't have rabies. But, if the cat is tested for rabies, then he will have to have the regular shots in the stomach," said Ricky's father. The father's explanation didn't matter to the lady and the others with her. To them, they only saw a tall, big man holding a dead cat that he killed and his little boy sobbing because of it.

Because of that, the father was seen as a villain in the neighborhood by some people, and some people would make comments like, "keep your cat away from him. He is gun crazy and looking to shoot helpless animals." And, when someone's pet would go missing, someone would usually say that Ricky's dad had shot the poor creature for sport. Most people knew though that the coyotes in the area were responsible for most of the missing cats. However, there were other neighbors who said Ricky's dad did the right thing.

So, Ricky's parents gave the dead cat to the Animal Control Service, and they cut the head off the dead cat and sent it to the laboratory. The lab results came back that the cat did not have rabies; thus Ricky didn't have to start regular shots in the stomach.